EMILY DICKINSON

Marnie Pomeroy

GREENWICH EXCHANGE
LONDON

Greenwich Exchange, London

First published in Great Britain in 2003
All rights reserved

Emily Dickinson
© Marnie Pomeroy 2004

Printed and bound by Q3 Digital/Litho, Loughborough
Tel: 01509 213456
Typesetting and layout by Albion Associates, London
Tel: 020 8852 4646
Cover design by December Publications, Belfast
Tel: 028 90352059

Cover picture of Emily Dickinson from Getty Images / Hulton Archive

Greenwich Exchange Website: www.greenex.co.uk

ISBN 1-871551-68-4

with thanks to Warren Hope

Other books by Marnie Pomeroy include:

A Practical Guide to Writing Poetry (1997)
The Speck (1972)
For Us Living (1970)
Soft Jobs and Miracles (1969)
A Calendar for Dinah (1966)

CONTENTS

Chronology

1830 Emily Elizabeth Dickinson born 10th December, at the Homestead on Main Street in Amherst, Massachusetts, to Emily Norcross Dickinson and Edward Dickinson (married 1828).
Older brother, William Austin Dickinson, had been born 1829.

1833 Sister, Lavinia (Vinnie) Norcross Dickinson, born.

1835 Father appointed treasurer of Amherst College (founded 1821). Austin and Emily attend Primary School.

1838 Emily first taken to church, which she attends until about 1861. The Dickinsons move to West Street (some say North Pleasant) where they live for 17 years.

1840 Emily and Vinnie attend Amherst Academy. Emily in a classics curriculum for seven years.

1842 Austin attends Williston Seminary. Emily's first-known letter written to him there.

1844 Emily's close friend and second cousin, Sophia Holland, dies at age 15. Emily allowed to visit at the time of her death; traumatised, she is sent to relatives in Boston and in Worcester for a month to recover.
Time of religious revival in Amherst.

1846 Austin attends Amherst College.

1847　Daguerreotype taken just after Emily's 16th birthday. Emily attends Mary Lyon's Female Seminary (Mount Holyoke).

1848　Emily brought home in the spring because of cough. After August she stays at home for health reasons. Law clerk, Benjamin Newton, opens her mind to new ideas and gives her confidence that she is a poet.
Death of Emily Brontë.

1849　Henry Wadsworth Longfellow's *Kavanagh* published.
Vinnie attends Ipswich boarding school.
Benjamin Newton leaves Amherst.
Death of Edgar Allan Poe.

1850　Emily's prose Valentine (mentioning her dog Carlo) written and published anonymously in Amherst College *Indicator*.
Writes first known poem, also a Valentine.
Friends include future sister-in-law, Susan (Sue) Gilbert.
Austin courts Sue, graduates from Amherst College, teaches one term at Sunderland, a few miles away.
Nathaniel Hawthorne's *The Scarlet Letter* published.

1851　Sue goes to Baltimore to teach. Austin teaching in Boston.
Father rings church bell one night to announce splendid aurora borealis.
Herman Melville's *Moby Dick* published.

1852　Emily's Valentine published anonymously in *Springfield Daily Republican*.
Austin home, finished with teaching.
Father, a Whig, elected Representative to 33rd Congress.

1853　Austin to Harvard Law School. Engagement to Sue.
Benjamin Newton dies, mourned by Emily.
Emily meets writer and literary editor of *Springfield Daily Republican*, Dr Holland, and his wife Elizabeth, who becomes a close friend.

Railroad, promoted by father, brought to Amherst.
Father in Washington, D.C.

1854 Death of Charlotte Brontë.
Austin graduates from Harvard Law School.

1855 Emily and Vinnie in Washington visiting Father, and in Philadelphia where Emily probably heard the Reverend Charles Wadsworth's sermons.
Father and Austin in law partnership.
Family moves back to the Homestead. Beginning of mother's invalidism.
Walt Whitman's *Leaves of Grass* published.

1856 Austin and Sue married; move into Evergreens next to the Homestead.
Emily's bread wins second prize at Agricultural Fair.
Uproarious social evenings at Evergreens, where Emily meets, among others over time, Samuel Bowles, editor of *Springfield Daily Republican.*

1858 Ralph Waldo Emerson, lecturing in Amherst, is entertained at Evergreens.
Austin has typhoid fever.
First letter to 'Master' composed. Emily starts writing a large number of poems secretly collected in fascicles.

1859 Evenings at Evergreens continue. Friend of Sue recalls Emily improvising "weird and beautiful melodies" on the piano.

1860 Wadsworth, staying with friends nearby, calls on Emily with whom he has been corresponding.
Abraham Lincoln elected President.

1861 Second Master letter, showing a time of crisis for Emily.
The Civil War begins 12th April.
Birth of Edward (Ned) to Sue and Austin.
Death of Elizabeth Barrett Browning.

Sue comments to Emily on the poem, 'Safe in their alabaster chambers'.

1862　Third Master letter.

Frazar Stearns, son of college president, killed in the Civil War.

Emily's first letter to Thomas Wentworth Higginson in response to his 'Letter to a Young Contributor' in the *Atlantic Monthly*.

Charles Wadsworth and his family move to San Francisco.

Death of Henry Thoreau.

Emily writes somewhere around 227 poems.

1863　Lincoln's Emancipation Proclamation – freeing all slaves.

Emily estimated to have written 295 poems.

1864　Emily in Boston for treatment from eye doctor from April to November, staying with cousins, Louisa and Frances Norcross.

Austin, drafted, buys substitute for $500.

Death of Nathaniel Hawthorne.

Lincoln re-elected President.

1865　Emily returns to Boston for eye treatment, April to October.

The Civil War ends 9th April.

President Lincoln shot five days later, dies 15th April.

Emily writes around 229 poems this year.

1866　Death of Emily's dog, Carlo.

Martha (Mattie) born to Sue and Austin.

Emily writes very few poems between 1866 and 1870.

1869　Wadsworth and family return to Philadelphia.

Emily writes to Higginson, refusing to visit him, stating that she does not cross her father's ground to any house or town.

1870　Higginson visits Emily.

1871　George Eliot's *Middlemarch* published.

1873 Higginson visits Emily again.
First evidence – an envelope addressed to her – of Judge Otis Lord's special friendship with Emily, formed while he and his wife had been to the Homestead on and off for years.

1874 Father dies in Boston.

1875 Mother partially paralysed; needs nursing by Emily and Vinnie for seven years.
Thomas Gilbert (Gib) born to Sue and Austin.
Otis Lord elevated to Massachusetts Supreme Court.

1876 Helen Hunt Jackson ('H.H.'), author of *Ramona*, writes to Emily that she is "a great poet", and tries to persuade her to publish.

1877 Bowles visits Emily, now habitually unapproachable. He shouts upstairs, "Emily, you Damned Rascal ... come down at once!" She did, and was never more fascinating, according to Vinnie.
Judge Lord's wife dies.

1878 Death of Samuel Bowles.
Emily's poem, 'Success is counted sweetest', attributed to Emerson.
Emily protected by Vinnie from knowledge of terrible fire in Amherst.

1880 Wadsworth's surprise (and last) visit. ("I stepped from my Pulpit to the Train.")
Judge Lord at the Homestead; romance with Emily most likely established.
Running water installed in the Homestead.

1881 Mabel Loomis Todd, wife of new astronomy teacher at Amherst College, entertained at Evergreens.
President Garfield shot.

1882 Death of Charles Wadsworth.
      Deaths of both Emerson and Longfellow.
      Austin and Mabel Todd begin love affair.
      Death of Mother.

1883 Death of Sue and Austin's son, Thomas Gilbert (Gib), aged
      eight.
      Matthew Arnold lectures in Amherst.

1884 Death of Judge Lord.
      Emily collapses in first attack of final illness.

1885 Emily confined to bed, cared for mostly by Vinnie.

1886 Death of Emily Dickinson, 15th May.

1890 *Poems, First Series*, edited by T.W. Higginson and Mabel
      Loomis Todd, published by Roberts Brothers, Boston. (11
      editions printed by the end of 1892.)

1891 *Poems, Second Series*, edited by T.W. Higginson and Mabel
      Loomis Todd (Roberts Brothers, Boston).

1894 *Letters*, edited by Mabel Loomis Todd, published.

1955 First text based on manuscripts published, edited by Thomas
      H. Johnson: *The Poems of Emily Dickinson, Including Variant
      Readings Critically Compared with All Known Manuscripts.*

1958 *The Letters of Emily Dickinson* published, edited by Thomas
      H. Johnson and Theodora Ward.

1981 *The Manuscript Books of Emily Dickinson* published, edited
      by R.W. Franklin.

Introduction

If I read a book [and] it makes my whole body so cold no fire
ever can warm me I know *that* is poetry. If I feel physically as
if the top of my head were taken off, I know *that* is poetry.
                                        (E.D. quoted by T.W. Higginson)

Emily Dickinson (1830 – 1886) wrote at the last count 1,789 poems.
Never did such an explosive body of work come in such small
packages. In her concision she contrasts quite perfectly with her
contemporary, the larger-than-life Walt Whitman, whose poems she
never read because she heard that "he was disgraceful". Her poetry,
despite unevenness and flaws, already speaks to us more strongly
than that of other Victorians such as Tennyson and the Brownings.
(We don't count Wordsworth's last years.) She would be a star in
any gathering.

Although 15 years old when she mentioned in a letter how "young
ladies aim to be poetical nowadays", the first poem she saved dates
from when she was 20. Two years later she began again with one a
year, soon increasing to a crescendo of quantity in 1862, 1863, and
1865. The poems then subsided, with two poems written the year
she died and many remaining undated. If there were lulls after those
three years of astonishing output, poetry of power still kept surfacing
throughout her œuvre.

Many of Dickinson's poems here are quoted (with several
adjustments) from James Reeves' selection because he edited them
without her distracting idiosyncrasies, such as an abundance of
dashes, which would have been regularised had she published. Others,
based on R.W. Franklin's collection of poems that are as near as
possible to her manuscripts, are similarly edited for clarity. As few
poems were ever titled, they are referred to when necessary by their
first lines.

Much anthologised, the three early poems that follow illustrate
her compact style, clarity, and strength that is sometimes surprisingly
violent. In this first, from her 28th year, her mature power begins to
show:

As if I asked a common alms,
And in my wondering hand
A stranger pressed a kingdom,
And I, bewildered, stand –
As if I asked the Orient
Had it for me a morn,
And it should lift its purple dikes,
And shatter me with dawn!

Note Dickinson's poetic licence here – the main subject and verb are never missed, only implied (*It is as if* ...). "Wondering", although assigned only to the outstretched hand, conjures up a whole person. "The Orient" refers to the geographical east, source of exotic treasure, as well as to the cardinal point where the sky is a vast purple sea. Its dikes, opening like a gift box, release an unexpected deluge of treasure in dawn's brilliant reds. As the word for making an impact on the viewer, "shatter" cannot be bettered. ("Dawn" partakes of the hardness of "dikes" through the alliterated *d*, adding to its ability to shatter.)

Ballad-metre quatrains are typical of Dickinson, and here she has run two of them together. The relaxed rhymes are also typical; working out exact ones would have been time consuming and run the risk of straining the sense and natural flow.

The next two poems were written the following year:

Water is taught by thirst,
Land by the oceans passed,
Transport by throe,
Peace by its battles told,
Love by memorial mold,
Birds by the snow.

The first line, a complete thought and so simple as to be elemental, contains enough poetry for the whole poem. Those that follow – rather like afterthoughts making this an official poem – show further examples of compression. The last line, somewhat anticlimactic after the dynamic human dimensions of those before, suggests in four words all of summertime as represented by birds, blanked out under endless, level, white winter.

Aside from one extra beat at the start of the second stanza in a three-beat-per-line pattern, the imperfect rhyming of "today" and "victory", and the inverted "So clear of Victory", this third poem is tightly written and sure as an arrow:

Success is counted sweetest
By those who ne'er succeed.
To comprehend a nectar
Requires sorest need.

Not one of all the purple host
Who took the flag today
Can tell the definition
So clear of victory

As he defeated, dying,
On whose forbidden ear
The distant strains of triumph
Burst agonized and clear.

Dickinson brings in the out-of-context "nectar" to make a sly pun on "sweetest". (Note the word "purple" again, here meaning 'royal'.) The theme is the same as the previous: Contrast heightens meaning. In the climax, note how the two strenuous words, "burst" and "agonized", together reinforce each other. Showing how highly it was thought of, this poem was attributed to Ralph Waldo Emerson when published anonymously in 1878.

If Emily Dickinson seems an unlikely major poet (frail, and born into a prominent family in a puritan New England town) she escaped all of her restrictions in a most unlikely way: through being reclusive. Her niece told of how she once led her up to her bedroom where, pretending to lock herself in, she turned an invisible key, saying that all it took was one turn and then … freedom!

With her tough Yankee attitude, and by writing poems alone in that bedroom, she got through midnight moments and then beyond into the bliss of being alive:

Oh sumptuous moment
Slower go
That I may gloat on thee –

1

Life In The Family

Gautier de Caen accompanied William the Conqueror from Normandy to England where his name was anglicised as Walter de Kenson. Dickinsons, his descendents, were Emily's forebears – well educated, enterprising, public spirited, and influential – who left Lincolnshire for America around 1636 in order to practice Puritanism. In 1759, they finally settled in what was to be Amherst, Massachusetts (named for Lord Jeffrey Amherst, whose idea it was to give the Indians smallpox-infected blankets). Emily's father's father became one of the founders of Amherst College, its main purpose at first being to train Evangelical ministers, a fire-and-brimstone antidote to the watering down of Protestantism by Unitarianism.

Seventy-five miles west of Boston, the country town of Amherst evolved as a centre for education. Inhabited and visited by highly cultivated people, it was assured contact with some of America's finest minds. (Ralph Waldo Emerson, for one, lectured there several times.) Having graduated from Yale, Emily's father, Edward Dickinson, served as treasurer of Amherst College and led the community while he practiced law. He also spent one term in the House of Representatives in Washington, D.C. Emily mentioned that he read only on Sunday – lonely and rigorous books. In letters she wrote, "Father steps like Cromwell when he gets the Kindlings", and "His heart was pure and terrible, and I think no other like it exists". Another side to him was shown in her letter of 1851 telling about great excitement one night: Her father's violent ringing of the church bell brought people rushing outdoors to witness the spectacular northern lights.

There is not much to say with certainty about her mother, Emily Norcross, whose father, also a benefactor of education, prospered as the most powerful citizen in nearby Monson. Because schooling for girls was interrupted when they were needed at home, Norcross' undeveloped written expression shows as drudgery in the few letters that remain. She preferred visiting or sending thoughtful little gifts. She was loved by many, and though her life was unexceptional it was not unproductive. Distinguished people were entertained in her household, and she taught Emily good housekeeping skills. The interest in flowers she gave young Emily was to last and be featured throughout her life. Although she couldn't be her confidante, she provided a matrix for the poet to develop in emotional warmth, privacy, and at leisure – a contribution that cannot be overestimated. She had an odd sense of humour shared by her namesake daughter, and a quiet presence diminished progressively by ill health. But whereas seclusion for the mother meant narrowing down, for her daughter it led to looking outward far and deep.

The marriage appears to have been based on a happy imbalance, and the whole family stayed close. When they grew up, Emily and her younger sister, Lavinia, remained always at home. Their older brother, Austin, established his family in the house next door built for him by their father, and joined him in his law practice.

Traditionally the men protected and guided the women. Emily greatly respected and loved her remote, authoritarian father even if she feared him. He had determined to be the best parent he could, applying a book's formula for successful child rearing: "You must provide a pleasant and happy home". Being delicate, shy, and high-strung, Emily was carefully sheltered. Though her father seemed overly solicitous, to catch a cold meant possible death. Many family members and friends lost children – sometimes all of them – and died young themselves.

Because of her shaky health, Emily's formal schooling was inconsistent, and tutoring by her mother may account for her lapses in proper writing. What she learned, however, she retained. By age 11 she was a precocious student remarked for wit and wordplay, with schoolmates crowding around her as she improvised original, funny stories. A friend also remembered from those days that Emily "loved with all her might". Her letters from this time are fluent and overwhelmingly affectionate and, as she grew up, sparkled with fun shared by Austin and Vinnie. At the same time she kept high standards:

"You know how I hate to be common", she wrote, always eager to get the highest marks and to be "the best little girl" as she had been told to be, though this came easily. Later, she rebelled in an unassailable way – she turned inwards.

Earlier, she had rebelled in another way. During the phenomenon known as 'The Great Awakening', Calvinist religion and Revivalism dominated Amherst. Alan Tate, the American poet and critic, observed that the Protestant ethic dramatised the human soul. Because of the sin of Adam and Eve, those not among the few 'elect' – the saved – were damned before birth to hell's eternal fires. Therefore, everyone was exhorted to join the ranks of the saved, though Edward Dickinson was more interested in his children's health and education than their piety. At school, where Revivalism was in full force, friends and teachers worked hard to manipulate Emily, one of the few holdouts, into declaring herself a saved Christian. Although friendly, the pressure was kept up against her in school, in 'praying circles', and in private. A strong character was needed to stand up for personal truth against the tide, especially as scepticism (Emily's bias) has not the heft of conviction. Through the years, one by one, her friends, then her brother declared themselves saved, and, most unexpectedly, even her father; but never Emily. One reason was that she could not accept the doctrine of original sin.

As a result she suffered. Excluded from the religious community, she expressed longing in an early letter not to be shut out from "this depth and fullness", ardently wishing for the event that had renewed the others. God was another matter: She was to refer to him in such sarcastic terms as an Eclipse addressed every morning by the religious members of her family. Belief in the life of the spirit, however, always informed her poems.

With a background of religious concern, where rigours allowed no excesses, Emily had as her example those virtues of her forebears – high-mindedness, honesty, fortitude, independence, hard work, thrift, and simplicity. They show in her poems. Similarly, New England architecture (such as the plain, white-clapboard churches with their small spires) and the elegant but unpretentious furniture of the times reflected the quality of the people. Despite a fragile constitution, the iron in Emily's character enabled her to survive grievous disappointment and the anguish caused by the many deaths around her, emerging with strength and renewal.

As a matter of course, she grew up exposed to the outstanding lectures and written works of Amherst's academic world, particularly to do with natural science. The vocabulary of the law also took hold as she witnessed legal documents for her father from age 12 onwards. But the Evangelical preachers, looked up to somewhat, like austere rock stars, whose sermons were the community's chief entertainment, probably drove home most for Emily the tremendous power of language.

Life at home included literary friends and visitors, as well as books and discussions about them. Besides periodicals, she had choice reading matter: Emerson and Thoreau (fellow New Englanders), both Brownings, Tennyson, Longfellow, George Herbert, Wordsworth, Sir Thomas Browne, Keats, and Shakespeare (she thought no other book was needed after reading him). Inevitably she knew the Bible, singling out Revelations when asked what she read. Because their father disapproved of current fiction, Austin had to smuggle Longfellow's novel, *Kavanagh*, into the house and hide it under the piano cover to share with her. She is thought to have modelled her relationship with Susan Gilbert, her future sister-in-law, on its portrayal of two girls in love with each other, writing impassioned letters as she did to Sue.

Emily had an intense visual sense, therefore paintings were important to her. She grew up familiar with reproductions of William Holman Hunt's 'The Light of the World' and landscapes of the Hudson River School, and had read John Ruskin's art criticism:

> These are the visions flitted Guido,
> Titian never told;
> Domenichino dropped his pencil,
> Paralyzed with gold.

With a painter's eye she applied bright colours to her poems – yellow, purple, red, blue, pink, silver, gold – like a child. (Black and white were for different or symbolic effects.) Often her small, colourful poems give an impression of word pictures drawn with crayons:

> Ample make this bed;
> Make this bed with awe.
> In it wait till judgment break
> Excellent and fair.

Be its mattress straight;
Be its pillow round;
Let no sunrise' yellow noise
Interrupt this ground.

A grave is simply a bed – its rounded headstone, a pillow. In the unusual "yellow noise", the sun's rays grow with the noise of the waking world. Emily occasionally took chances ahead of her time by pairing sight with sound.

She was also musical, writing of birds that " ... stab my ravished spirit/ With dirks of melody". An accomplished player of the piano, she developed a gift for improvisation. In the happy, early days of Austin's marriage to Susan Gilbert, a friend of Sue remembered hearing Emily's "weird and beautiful melodies" at one of the social gatherings in her brother's house before she withdrew from society. When the sensational soprano Jenny Lind, "the Swedish Nightingale", sang in Northampton, the Dickinsons attended (though nobody was much impressed). In school Emily had taken great pleasure in singing with others and, most likely having the classical Greeks in mind, frequently wrote about singing as synonymous with writing poetry. There may have been a connection between this and her using the verse forms of ballads and of hymns she had sung.

After day-school (begun at age five) Emily spent her last eight school-years irregularly. At Amherst Academy, inspiring, college-level lectures were open to any student, and later, thanks to them, words such as 'perihelion' and 'parallax' came naturally to her. Following that, for most of one school year she boarded at Mount Holyoke Female Seminary. The curricula in both institutions were enlightened, if tipped towards religious interpretation. Her courses included Latin – she translated several books from the *Aeneid* before dropping it – English, mathematics, natural sciences, philosophy, and singing. In 1848, however, just when Emily's homesickness was tempered by enthusiasm for the new courses at boarding school, her father heard that she had contracted a persistent cough, and sent Austin to fetch her home despite her great reluctance. After being dosed by her father's medicines, she returned healthy to finish the school year before going home for good in August.

With fields, woods, and hills close by, the streets of Amherst were lined by trees, and the large, handsome houses had adjoining gardens also shaded by plenty of trees. The Dickinson's original house on Main Street, known as 'The Homestead', or 'The Mansion', was the most imposing of all. When Emily had been nine years old, the Dickinsons moved to another on West Street, slightly less grand but greatly loved, the one Emily returned to now. Despite carved mahogany furniture and elaborate silverware within – Emily Norcross' dowry hauled to Amherst from Monson by yoked oxen – housework always included drawing water from a well, and tending fireplaces and woodstoves. Unless the laundry was done by servants, it had to be sent out. Gentlewomen both sewed and employed seamstresses. (The poem 'Don't put up my thread and needle' is all about sewing). Nevertheless, tasks were easier than for Emily's paternal grandmother, who once excused the brevity of a letter because that day they were busy killing hogs.

Emily helped with housework and learned to cook, specialising in desserts, while continuing to write letters to her old friends. She also enjoyed the company of her brother's literary classmates for two years after her return home – then they graduated from Amherst College with Austin. But, most importantly, Benjamin Newton, a young law student in her father's office, introduced her to Emerson's poems among others, and to new thoughts including a concept of immortality apart from Calvinism. He died of tuberculosis a few years after leaving Amherst in 1849, having given her the greatest gift of all – the intoxicating idea that she, herself, was a poet.

"Amherst is alive with fun this winter", she wrote in one letter of 1850, missing Austin away at Harvard Law School, and his "big Hurrahs and the famous stir". Aside from the usual (maple) sugaring parties, she reported a sleigh ride on a grand scale, a frolic comprising charades, music, conversation, and supper "set in the most modern style", a sliding party, several cosy sociables, a party "universale", and one "confidentiale". But she was kept busy with chores and the next year she complained to Austin that there weren't many jokes now, it was mostly sobriety – that "we do not have much poetry, father having made up his mind that it's pretty much all real life".

Emily's news of family in letters to Austin habitually included livestock – chickens, later a lone turkey, the cats, and especially the horse. In 1849, her father gave her a puppy, Carlo, who was to be her companion for 16 years and mentioned with great fondness in letters and poems. See how this dog image represents her distress at not receiving a longed-for letter:

> What shall I do, it whimpers so –
> This little hound within the heart,
> All day and night with bark and start ...

And how fitting this is, in the concluding stanza of a later poem:

> Adventure most unto itself
> The soul condemned to be,
> Attended by a single hound –
> Its own identity.

In many ways her father's ideas were old-fashioned even for those times, going beyond the protection of women. He believed that they should stay home, not have a vote, and furthermore, be discreet enough not to let their written words circulate in public. When a wild-spirited, anonymous prose Valentine, rightly attributed to Emily, was published in 1850 in Amherst College's literary monthly, she must have heard from her father that this was not to happen again.

The earliest of her poems that we have is another exuberant Valentine, 40 lines long, written in couplets with an uncharacteristic six beats per line and a pause in the middle of each. It begins:

> Awake ye muses nine, sing me a strain divine,
> Unwind the solemn twine, and tie my Valentine!

Never at a loss for words, she handled her derivative material skilfully.

The next few years were critical for her. Literary young men like Newton had established her sense of herself as a poet. She met Susan Gilbert who was to become her best friend, marry her brother, and remain an appreciative recipient of a number of her poems. (At that time there was a shared sense of fun: Emily wrote to her brother of how she and Sue "sat and screamed" with laughter at his facetious letter.) In 1855, when her father served in the House of Representatives, she visited Washington D.C., then Philadelphia.

In Philadelphia, she evidently heard the sermons of the Reverend Charles Wadsworth. With his deep voice, charismatic oratory, and tragic air, he was a romantic figure who impressed both believers and non-believers, including Mark Twain. We know that Emily Dickinson wrote to him asking for spiritual guidance because his undated answer was preserved. We also know that he visited her twice, and that they corresponded in secret for about seven years until he moved to San Francisco, and then again after his return seven years later until he died. Even though happily married, 16 years older than she, and a former poet who came to publicly decry poetry, evidence favours him as the man she considered herself married to in soul.

Supposing that he was her beloved, we may speculate that nothing of love was ever actually said between them although each may have recognised strong feelings – theirs, or just hers. While continuous correspondence indicates mutual interest, Dickinson may have read more into Wadsworth's letters than he intended or suspected. Yet, after his death, a close friend of his sent her a collection of his sermons and corresponded with her about him. Something of substance that was concealed seems to have existed.

Following the trip to Washington D.C. and Philadelphia, the Dickinson family moved from the West Street house back to the remodelled Homestead, more grand than ever, where Emily was to stay until she died, leaving only twice to have her eyes treated in Boston.

She had suffered intolerance to light and severe pain in her eyes, and often feared that she was going blind. The diagnosis of the day was "rheumatic iritis", the treatment painful, with no reading allowed, and the outcome completely successful. During those long, darkened months of treatment she was read to by her cousins with whom she stayed. It was then that she discovered the glories of Shakespeare's *Antony and Cleopatra*.

Next door in their Amherst villa, called The Evergreens (built for them by his father), Austin and his wife Sue began marriage together in 1856, involving Emily in many aspects. For a few years Emily was still circulating in Amherst society, winning prizes for her bread at the cattle show, and spending many evenings with Austin and Sue and their friends. Although there is no record of Emily meeting him there, Ralph Waldo Emerson stayed at The Evergreens after giving one of his popular lectures.

A frequent visitor, mostly without his wife, was Samuel Bowles. While privately pulling strings to determine the politics of the day in Massachusetts and in Washington, D.C., he was owner and editor-in-chief of the *Springfield Republican*, one of the most influential newspapers in the United States. Magnetic and high-powered, he became one of Emily's most important friends, and some have considered him a candidate for Emily's secret love. Though a man with national connections, and who travelled abroad, it would seem from the number of letters he wrote Austin and Sue, and the discussions with Sue about his being occasionally tempted by women, that he considered them his best friends. His nephew once made a list of the six women he considered dynamite: Emily and Sue were among them.

Austin was handsome in the craggy New England way, something of a dandy, and, as a lawyer, a great catch. His marriage to Sue – smart, glamorous, manipulative, very socially ambitious, and probably charming – turned out to be a big mistake. While he preferred quiet, she wanted to entertain, making a point of snaring all the important visitors to Amherst, and running the house as a sort of salon. Also, she did not enjoy making love, which was perhaps connected with her terror of pregnancy. (One of her sisters had died of puerperal fever and another had lost her first child.) In time Austin responded to an adoring, much younger woman (by 27 years), Mabel Loomis Todd, married to an astronomer newly hired to direct the Amherst College Observatory. They had a passionate affair that lasted until Austin's death in 1895.

It was said that Emily's naturally curly auburn hair, straightened somewhat to suit the puritan fashion, was beautiful; that she had dark eyes, white skin, and an attractive, soft voice. Having no photograph to send at the request of Thomas Wentworth Higginson, the writer with whom she corresponded, she wrote him this self-portrayal: "I ... am small, like the Wren, and my Hair is bold, like the Chestnut Bur – and my eyes, like the Sherry in the Glass, that the Guest leaves". Later she compared herself to bluebirds, which "do their work just like me. They dart around just so, with little dodging feet, and look so agitated".

Congenial people enjoyed her quick wit and droll joking. Intelligence is everywhere in her work, but perhaps it was her naïve quality that precluded a polished technique. Emily thought of herself as a child, a little one; we find this in many poems. At times she even called herself a boy. This really meant a tomboy – an undomesticated girl freed of formalised self; someone young and small enough to cherish, indulge, and protect in her vulnerability; an innocent whose primal and irregular experiences can be winked at; someone cheeky, muddy, sunburned, and barefoot. In letters and poems she refers to being barefoot.

The German philosopher, Artur Schopenhauer, remarked that a genius always remains a big child, and this was manifest in Emily. While it suited her physical type, she may have also wanted to stay childlike in proportion to her father's dominance. Doubtlessly it helped her handle him – fostering his protectiveness and insuring his affection. She retained the dynamics of that relationship with some other men important to her, keeping up the pretence that Higginson was a mentor, seeing herself as subordinate to (and at the mercy of) the Master of her three 'Master letters', and later finding mutual love with an arch-authority-figure – an intimidating, though charming judge 18 years her senior.

As her twenties passed, Emily must have found herself lonelier with people than when alone. Her sister, Vinnie, explained her withdrawal as "a happen". It seemed that she just gradually stopped going out rather than that she deliberately withdrew. Her intensity must have made her hard to be with, and the overpowering affection, as shown in her early letters, would have been impossible to return. As she matured, her shyness may have become more like hopelessness of being herself with those not close to her. Frustrated with people, who in time also distracted her from her business of enlightened living, she gradually stopped going out. This was not a choice, but self-preservation. Her temperament precluded casual dealings with others, and the magnitude of actual contact overcharged her inner world extreme with its climates of rapture and despair. She was best served by solitude. Anthony Storr, an eminent psychiatrist, stated that solitude (like art) allows control and integration. Alone, Emily could protect her balance and integrity. While letters connected her to others, writing poems was her lifeline to meaning. Out of the small verse format, set within a restricted material life "too simple and stern to embarrass any", her poetic life expanded like a genie swelling from a bottle. Only after her death was it known how many poems she had written in secret.

The American Civil War (1861-1865), the most agonized and significant event America has experienced, was not particularly remarked by many Northerners. Emily's reaction, as judged by some of her quoted remarks, seems to have been a deliberate distancing, such as in refusing to make bandages. And, as an accepted means of avoiding military service, Austin Dickinson paid $500 for a substitute to serve in his place.

When three young men from Amherst – one a good friend of Austin, the son of the president of Amherst College, and both sons of an old family friend – joined the army and were killed, the shock was felt hard by the whole Dickinson family, particularly Austin. Also touching upon Emily's life was that Higginson, in charge of the first regiment of ex-slaves, was wounded, although not seriously. Again as a poet contrasted with Emily Dickinson, Walt Whitman, now too old to fight for the Union, volunteered for hospital service. He prevented many amputations, besides nursing those who had suffered them and others who were wounded and dying.

War is known to stimulate creative energies, and this was borne out in Emily's case. That she was deep in a personal hell around this time is seen by her drafts of the second and third 'Master letters'. Although not ever inclined to care about politics (" … 'George Who?' That sums all Politics to me.") she was nevertheless aware that this war pressed upon her sense of mortality as well as her personal dilemmas, and that it energised her poetic development:

> I heard as if I had no ear
> Until a vital word
> Came all the way from life to me
> And then I knew I heard;
>
> I saw as if my eye were on
> Another, till a thing –
> And now I know 'twas light because
> It fitted them – came in;

I dwelt as if myself were out,
My body but within,
Until a Might detected me
And set my kernel in;

And Spirit turned into the dust:
"Old Friend, thou knowest me!"
And Time went out to tell the news
And met Eternity.

Henry Thoreau, who recommended "self-reliance, plain living, and high thinking", may have inspired this poem with two lines of his own, from *A Week on the Concord and Merrimack Rivers*: "I hearing get, who had but ears,/ And sight, who had but eyes before …" This would not have been plagiarism, but a common-enough imprinting of one poet's work upon another's psyche while Emily took in what she read and experienced, and poems streamed out of her. She is known to have found reading a rich source for her poems.

An ex-minister, Higginson had become active in literary fields. Emily, who had read his advice to writers in the *Atlantic Monthly*, wrote to ask his opinion about her enclosed poems. After they finally met, having corresponded for eight years, he described her in a letter to his wife: "a little plain woman", the face "with no good feature", and her voice, when she made her introduction by putting two daylilies into his hand, was soft, breathless, frightened, and like a child's. After commenting on her being ingenuous and childlike, but wise, he went on to say, "I never was with anyone who drained my nerve power so much. Without touching her, she drew from me. I am glad not to live near her. She often thought me tired & seemed very thoughtful of others". Decades after that, he recorded his impression of her giving off "an excess of tension, and of an abnormal life".

Judging by her earlier liveliness, one might consider Emily to have been partly a frustrated extrovert – forced into the background by her father's condemnation of women writers going public, by a lack of soulmates, and most of all by her own high-strung sensibilities. Her reclusive life was never absolute: Aside from her seeing immediate family, the constant rounds of letters sent and received show how affectionately engaged she was with others.

Vinnie, pert, pretty, and never lacking for beaux, remained unmarried, devotedly at her side with Emily deeply dependent upon her. The pert grew into the peppery as her sharp tongue became fearsome in the village. Designated social manager, she shielded Emily from outsiders and protected her in all ways she could. During Amherst's most terrible fire, she came into Emily's room "soft as a moccasin" and told her that it was only the Fourth of July, which Emily chose to believe despite some scepticism. She shared what was comical with Emily, and entertained family and guests at many dinners as an outstanding mimic. No writer herself, she delighted in Emily's way with words (as did the whole family), and declared Emily "the thinker" for all of them. We can believe her when she confided to someone that Emily turned down suitors, saying, "I have never seen anyone I cared for as much as you, Vinnie."

Their father lived until 1874, and their mother, 1882, having been ill and nursed by Emily and Vinnie through her last seven years. There was also domestic help, and very occasionally Emily accepted a visitor. She did not always keep indoors. One of her letters states: "I do not go away but the grounds are ample – almost travel – to me". Always fond of children, from time to time she would lower a basket full of gingerbread from her window to those who played nearby. And once, when her nephew left his boots at her house, she had them returned full of flowers on a silver tray. She developed a persona and became a kind of myth in Amherst. Even those who didn't read poetry knew that she wrote it, and they gossiped about her being a recluse always dressed in white. Protectively, her family closed ranks and refused to discuss her.

The wearing of white could have had many interpretations. She was a bride of a forever absent lover, or a votive virgin of the spiritual life, or a priestess of poetry, putting on a daily uniform to augment her role the way John Keats dressed carefully before working for the Muse. Or just plain comfortable in her version of a house gown. Alfred Habegger, her recent biographer, who saw her one surviving dress (relatively informal despite tucks and lace edging), pointed out that white was far easier to wash than more formal garb coloured with unstable dyes. Today, her white dress has become part of her cult, with women wearing white photographed in Emily-Dickinsonesque poses next to garden flowers.

Although Emily may have given up the idea of marriage because the first man she loved was out of reach, or because she wanted to dedicate herself to poetry, her childlike physique possibly contributed to her destiny in this regard. Marriage implied childbirth. Not without hazards even for the robust, for a woman with her constitution it could well have been disastrous.

Conjectures about her sexual bias persist with nothing proven. The passion expressed in letters written to Sue, her sister-in-law – undeniably love letters – must also be seen in the light of her temperament, of the sentimental friendships cultivated by women at that time, and of this being a chance to practice writing prose. No less deniable was her passion for the first man she loved, and her relationship with Judge Otis Lord towards the end of their lives. Sue, dropping by one day, found Emily in her drawing room reclining in the arms of a man.

Around 1880 (possibly a year or two prior) she became romantically involved with the Judge, who had been a close friend of her father and who was one of the most distinguished men in Massachusetts. Despite shared linguistic pleasures and passionate feelings she refused to marry him, and four years later he died. Emily had seemed to keep her equilibrium throughout family disruptions, but the heartbreak from so many deaths of those most dear to her was wearing down her health.

The following poem, one of her most poignant, begins on a personal note and ends on a general in the two memorable lines. She wonders if dying can be anything as momentous as two devastations she had survived (we can only guess which ones she meant here), and she asserts in closing that heaven is known by our loss of it – referring to our primal loss of Eden besides all loss of what was loved:

> My life closed twice before its close.
> It yet remains to see
> If immortality unveil
> A third event to me,
>
> So huge, so hopeless to conceive
> As these that twice befell.
> Parting is all we know of heaven,
> And all we need of hell.

Her death in a coma at age 55 was ascribed to Bright's disease, a form of kidney degeneration, but as she showed no signs of uremic poisoning there were good reasons to doubt the doctor's diagnosis and to consider cumulative stress – "revenge of the nerves" – the cause. Those who saw her before her burial commented on how remarkably young she looked, with smooth skin and no grey in her auburn hair.

2

The Poet and her Poetry

That we are missing biographical facts, and the posthumous discovery of so many poems, have no doubt deepened Emily Dickinson's allure, but this ultimately rests on the quality of her poems. Higginson was intrigued by the relatively few he saw, but had many reservations and judged them overly idiosyncratic for publication. That he thought them "too delicate" reveals his blindness to their power and his failure to distinguish concision from small size. (Incidentally, the entire text of one of her letters, not to him, reads: "Area – no test of depth.")

Letters

Dickinson's letters should be read along with her poems for their frequent flashes of poetry. Unfortunately, most by far are lost. Writing and receiving them was Dickinson's social life, making possible the contact she craved yet could not otherwise tolerate. Like all interesting letters they are defined by qualities of mind, not events.

Those addressing someone called 'Master' constitute the centrepiece of her secret life. Found in draft form among her papers after her death, there are three. Their openness makes them painful to read. The personal and exposed quality in Dickinson's poems that wins people over is here without any cordoning off by poetic form. Disjointedly, if not brokenly, they express her torment in the hopeless love of a man, and her trying to hang on to a one-sided relationship through self-abasing promises. Reading them, one feels like a voyeur who ends up traumatised by the shock of proximity. (According to one theory, these letters were calculated for effect. Although we shouldn't make assumptions, such sustained deception seems totally alien to Dickinson as we know her.)

Finally, her poetry and prose are not particularly differentiated. In 1858, her letters – previously abundant, deluging the recipients with affection – became more measured and succinct (and, at times, precious). It was as if her baffled yearning for response was subsequently converted into a formidable engagement with language – expressing fondness, thanks, and condolence – whatever needed saying. She came to specialise in spare notes that pointed up the circumstance. If an elliptical phrase appears strained, closer reading may discover an enriched sense. These letters continued to maintain the arms' length friendships that she needed as such.

From this, to Samuel Bowles, we have a passage whose extended metaphor owes all to her familiar pantry:

> I hope your cups are full. I hope your vintage is untouched. In such a porcelain life, one likes to be sure that all is well, lest one stumble upon one's hopes in a pile of broken crockery.
>
> (August 1859)

She approached Thomas Higginson about her poetry in letters that have since become famous. From the first:

> Are you too deeply occupied to say if my Verse is alive?
> The Mind is so near itself – it cannot see, distinctly – and I
>   have none to ask –
> Should you think it breathed – and had you the leisure to tell
>   me, I should feel quick gratitude –
> If I make the mistake – that you dared to tell me – would give
>   me sincerer honor – toward you – ...
>
> (15th April 1862)

Her second letter to him is calculated to intrigue. These extracts follow a white lie saying that she'd written no poems but one or two until the past winter – when she'd written 271 by the end of the previous year:

> I had a terror – since September – I could tell to none – and so
>   I sing, as the Boy does by the Burying Ground – because I
> am afraid –
> ... I have a Brother and Sister – My Mother does not care for
>   thought – and Father, too busy with his Briefs – to notice

what we do – He buys me many Books – but begs me not
to read them – because he fears they joggle the Mind ...
Could you tell me how to grow – or is it unconveyed – like
Melody – or Witchcraft?

(25th April 1862)

The terror of September 1861, never explained, more or less
coincided with the time in which the second and third 'Master' letters
were written.

She explained in an explosion-and-fire metaphor to
Higginson, who evidently made suggestions about her poems:

I ... cannot rule myself, and when I try to organise – my little
force explodes – and leaves me bare and charred –

(August 1862)

Inspired by her letters and by her refusals to come to Boston to
see him, Higginson memorably outdid himself, writing to her:

I have the greatest desire to see you, always feeling that perhaps
if I could once take you by the hand I might be something to
you; but till then you only enshroud yourself in this fiery mist
& I cannot reach you, but only rejoice in the rare sparkles of
light.

(May 1869)

This, as close to poetry as prose can be, from Dickinson's
answering letter that invited him to Amherst:

A Letter always feels to me like immortality because it is the
mind alone without corporeal friend. Indebted in our talk to
attitude and accent, there seems a spectral power in thought
that walks alone.

(June 1869)

To Perez Cowan, a second cousin and a minister whose sister had
died, this definition of dying, a matchless compression:

... Dying is a wild Night and a new Road.

(October 1869)

After his visit, Higginson quoted Emily Dickinson to his wife in a letter, the same one in which he described her appearance:

> I find ecstasy in living – the mere sense of living is joy enough. I asked if she never felt want of employment, never going off the place & never seeing any visitor "I never thought of conceiving that I could ever have the slightest approach to such a want in all future time" (& added) "I feel that I have not expressed myself strongly enough."
>
> (August 1870)

Sad to say, there exist two examples of gentle backbiting by Higginson. To his sisters he restated his wife's remark on Emily, "Oh why do the insane so cling to you?" And later he referred to her as "my partially cracked poetess". He remained, however, a staunch friend, and who can say if her poems would ever have been published after her death without his influence?

To her beloved cousins, Louise and Frances Norcross, after her mother's death:

> I cannot see how eternity seems. It sweeps around me like a sea.
>
> (November, 1882)

And here is a bright note on which to end, to Mabel Loomis Todd, entire text:

> To the bugle every color is red.
>
> (May 1885)

Words and Lines

Being a poet starts with a tactile approach to language. Therefore, mention should be made of her handwriting, so improbably well-mimicked by the master-forger Mark Hofmann, and the best we have for dating many poems by its changes. Her script with its strong, thick strokes seems more painted than written. Simple, round, and enclosing, the letters slope forward, sometimes connecting, sometimes not. No letter's tail extends far or forcefully below the line, but *t*'s are often crossed with long and heavy slashes. Dickinson's promiscuous use of dashes and capital letters has been much debated, yet Richard Sewell, her first exhaustive biographer, had found a composition book taught from in Amherst Academy that noted contemporary writers' substituting the dash for almost all marks of punctuation; it also recommended beginning words with capital letters for emphasis, or for being the main subjects of the composition. Some think that Dickinson used dashes as a guide to reading the poems aloud. Perhaps her hand enjoyed releasing an irrelevant energy coming through as she wrote, just as it did in the vehement script itself.

With further respect to tactility, Dickinson stated to an old friend, "Now I don't know of anything so mighty [as words] … Sometimes I write one, and look at his outlines till he glows as no sapphire". (Note the personification.) And "A Word is inundation, when it comes from the Sea" (a place of mystery and depth). Once she excused herself from seeing a visitor because "my own words so chill and burn me, that the temperature of other Minds is too new an Awe – ".

Beginning with a love of words and respect for their roots (Anglo-Saxon, Latin, and Greek) she combined the everyday with the eclectic vocabularies of law and natural science. When she had to be read to after eye-treatments in Boston, *Antony and Cleopatra* fired up her appreciation of Shakespeare anew. Back home, she described herself flying to the shelves and devouring the luscious passages, thinking she would tear the leaves out as she turned them.

By hardly ever using adjectives, aside from 'little' and colour-words, she proved that good writing doesn't need decoration. In this next poem, "Overflowing" in qualifying "word" creates the poetry and, together with "little", suggests what is weepy with feeling – all the more so for the "word" never being named:

> A little overflowing word
> That any, hearing, had inferred
> For ardor or for tears,
> Though generations pass away,
> Traditions ripen and decay,
> As eloquent appears.

Here and there she experimented with word forms such as "terribler", "pangless", and "russetly", and sometimes used words in a novel way – "panting ankle", which is truly grotesque. Or one noun will stand for a phrase, such as "a dew" for a drop of dew; this works well, implying more dewiness – something smaller than the indiscriminate drop. (In the same poem, 'A bird came down the walk', we find "plashless".)

Although steeped in her favourite poetry written in the iambic pentameter, Dickinson expressed herself through short lines, often in what is called common metre (four-line stanzas with four, and three iambic feet – thus 4-3-4-3 – rhymed *abcb*, or *abab*. Perhaps this was partly the child in her, choosing the immediacy of the familiar – the verse forms in periodicals and hymns. One also thinks of 'Mother Goose', and especially of ballads. As well, she frequently used short metre: 3-3-4-3.

Because she broke up her verses, would avert obvious rhymes and the expected metre, and would even narrow a stanza to one word per line (the versions sent with letters differ), she is valued by some as an innovator, a prosodic rebel. It is more likely, however, that she was experimenting rather than thinking of herself as an innovator per se.

It is possible that she hardly ever allowed herself the deep breaths and long, free strides of the pentameter because she was not liberated in other ways. Short lines, however, granted her the concision of a fist. When clear and simple they deliver their essence person to person in little punches. Furthermore, they allow us to assimilate the aphoristic compression of her poetry as it goes along, where five-beat lines would have been too dense and slow.

Strangely, perhaps, the effect of writing about large geographical bodies or universal themes in short lines and small poems can be seen to increase their size. This is partly the Less-Is-More Principle where understatement performs the miracle. Also, the act of filling a frame with a subject, so that it takes up all the available space, gives convincing heft and stature almost regardless of the size of the frame or form. Dickinson's miniatures on infinity and eternity extend so far because the imagination is given space. The same distance is lost on a crammed page because long lines call attention to themselves. A word alone has no boundaries, whereas a sentence, qualifying it, does. See how lines with only one noun convey its scope:

> Exultation is the going
> Of an inland soul to sea,

Past the houses, past the headlands,
Into deep eternity.

Again and again Dickinson connected the sea with love, sex, death, and eternity.

Her odd grammatical constructions doubtlessly were to suit her own ends, such as approaching the reader in an oblique way through use of the subjunctive. By softening her assertions she could appear less provocative. (Ending a poem with a dash rather than a full stop expresses something tentative for all of its thrust.) In view of her force as a poet, it was no wonder that she wanted to hide within a child's persona in her particular society.

Criticisms

That Dickinson has come to be known as one of the most important American poets – indeed, one of the greatest writing in English – is all the more remarkable because she has been handicapped by pronounced literary faults. These need to be aired in the open. This way, they have a chance of being seen more like the flaws of a good friend.

Even today when almost anything can be called poetry, Dickinson has been criticised for rough versifying. This is a problem only if an expectation has been set up, then disappointed, by a changed metre or an off-rhyme. Ideally, nothing should impede the experience of a poem, which is always best absorbed through multiple readings anyway. If the poem gives pleasure, whatever roughness should lose its burr by becoming incorporated into the loved whole. If we deplore roughness, we might remember that smooth, perfect versification may lull us into ignoring weaknesses (as do preconceptions and a poet's fame). The same is true for cleverness, the glory and the bane of contrived poetry, which can be all flash and no warmth and therefore soon dead. At best, Dickinson's cleverness served to condense and sum up, not to make form perfect for its own sake. She didn't have the gift of facility; if she couldn't smooth a line, she left it – rightly giving the poetry first place. At worst, over-condensed ideas were made still more difficult if she inverted the syntax.

Opaque passages break the flow most of all. On their account she has been charged with obscurity (not to be confused with deliberate riddling or the mystery often intrinsic to poetry). This is a problem, and poems must earn their right to puzzle by being very good. Whereas one may indulge wrong spelling and grammar, wilful punctuation, askew rhymes, irregular metrics, and jarring inversions, passages that remain frustrating cannot be called successful, though this does not mean they need to translate into prose. Actually, some fine poetry that can't be strictly reasoned out is often intelligible when read slightly out of focus. (Making poetic sense is what we best live by.)

One of her most singular poems, 'My life had stood, a loaded gun', has provoked endless guesswork as to its meaning. The poem will probably always keep its secret. Readers have complained about the end, "For I have but the power to kill/ Without the power to die", which eliminates many happy guesses. And yet the poem forever intrigues with a life of its own. Perhaps the interpretation that hits nearest the mark (so to speak) is that of the American writer, J.V. Cunningham, suggesting "an internalised Satanism of the divided self".

Dickinson has been criticised as well for being unprofessional. Professionalism in the writing of lyric poetry is more an attitude, meaning you do your best. She seems to have done this, leaving the bulk of her 1,789 poems neatly stacked in packets or 'fascicles' (the term for a division of a book sewn together at the fold) and sets (unsewn sheaves) that she had made. Further revisions must have been intended, for many poems were still in draft stages, and others certainly would have been weeded out if printing were planned. The pressures of housework and keeping up with the flood of new poems seem to have made the ever-increasing backlog impossible to deal with. Eloquently, her project of entering poems carefully in the fascicles gave way using loose sets, then merely piling on what had been jotted down on any scrap of paper at hand.

In any case, writing lyric poetry is not a profession, but a by-product of experience and a love-affair with language. Most who make a profession out of what they call poetry are performers, and, sadly, today there is not enough strong poetry in these events. Shakespeare and Dante made professional use of their vehicles for poetry – drama and narrative. These elicited poetry from them in the process of being written, but poetry wasn't the aim; it was incidental, even if it turned out to be what has kept the works alive.

Her most irritating fault comes from an ingrained characteristic:

> I'm nobody. Who are you?
> Are you nobody too?
> Then there's a pair of us.
> Don't tell – they'd banish us, you know.
>
> How dreary to be somebody,
> How public – like a frog –
> To tell your name the livelong June
> To an admiring bog.

This is a good poem, neatly done and with a sharp point. But the humour in the first stanza becomes arch, conspiratorially cute. Another example from the poem 'Arcturus is his other name' takes it further:

> Perhaps the "kingdom of Heaven's" changed.
> I hope the "Children" there
> Wont be "new fashioned" when I come –
> And laugh at me – and stare!
>
> I hope the Father in the skies
> Will lift his little girl –
> "Old fashioned"! naughty! everything!
> Over the stile of "pearl"!

(This extract has been left as published from the manuscript to demonstrate the point.) Here we have High Twee, not unconnected with the childlike, bright-coloured pictures Emily Dickinson drew with words. Nor is it out of character for one who referred to herself as a little girl well into middle age, and with noticeable frequency used the word 'little'.

There is another stile image at the end of "I'll tell you how the sun rose", not with naughty little Emily going through the pearly gates, but as a delightful description of a sunset as children and not embarrassing or sentimental at all. (She knew Blake's 'Songs of Innocence'):

But how he set, I know not –
There seemed a purple stile
That little yellow boys and girls
Were climbing all the while,
Till when they reached the other side
A Dominie in gray
Put gently up the evening bars,
And led the flock away.

Women, always identified with children, are often appreciated for childlike qualities. Even today, some young women affect high voices or hang on to mannerisms of children such as a lisp, giggling, etc., with intent to defuse aggression and inspire sexual attraction. Being small and soft is feminine, as it is childlike. While men's qualities tend to lead them to discuss abstract topics, female qualities bring women closer to the human and little details of living. Just as self-importance is often a man's failing, so is silliness a woman's.

Written by a woman who both appeared and spoke of herself as childlike, Dickinson's poems carry a woman's traits through the years more unmistakably than can be accounted for by the contemporary diction. Whereas one may be embarrassed by what is arch in women's writing today – limp puns, an all-us-girls-together tone – so one finds the little girl in some of Dickinson's work, twee meeting stupendous. We have to continually remember that Dickinson never had to edit for publication. Judging by the many alternate versions she left, she had difficulty making those painful decisions. If she had thought that her manuscripts would survive after her death, she was leaving choices up to others. In fact, irregularities were smoothed over and even some of her words changed in the earliest editions of her poems. We can only hope that there was no censorship by destruction. Now, what we believe to be everything has been published as faithfully to the original as possible. An editor's having to designate and even construct many final versions is the outcome of Dickinson's not having done so.

In conclusion, we are the beneficiaries of an immense, irregular opus, able to choose which poems and which parts of poems to return to. Individually responsible for doing works of art justice by enjoying them, we may as well accept Dickinson's faults as part of the effort that made her poems possible.

Word Magic: Metaphor, and Personification

Description – or to put it better, embodiment – sometimes incidental to the message, is one of the functions and delights of poetry, and its element easiest to point out. In itself it is not enough to make a poem qualify for greatness – that would include the power to enter the heart and answer our need for serious meaning, something that deepens or enlightens experience. Good description, however, can dilate our sense of feeling alive and give us new eyes.

When the senses are open, as they are most in undamaged children and persons of genius, they interconnect, which explains why someone with one talent is probably many-talented. It also explains the startling physicality of Dickinson's images – how she animated what she saw by describing things in terms of other things.

Neuroscientists have reported from research using brain scans that people with synesthesia really do perceive colours when they hear words. Not that Dickinson really had synesthesia when she wrote: "The prism never held the hues,/ It only heard them play". And, in the poem 'I heard a fly buzz when I died', colour is used with sound to make poetry, suggesting the whole event of a bluebottle fly on the window – "With blue, uncertain, stumbling buzz".

It is now believed that the conditions for metaphor are created in the part of the brain where converging information from different senses crosses paths. When this arrangement becomes disrupted, a person is unable to understand metaphor. As if we hadn't guessed, poets who reproduce sensory experiences through words are the lucky ones who have kept the extra synapses with which they were born, and hence can perceive connections. Our concern here is to point out examples of what Dickinson saw.

Whether poets believe that poetry is inspired or contrived, they often have to find a right word to quicken their subject. If that word turns out to be a congruous modifier (corresponding in character or kind), so that their notion wears a glorious but appropriate dress, the result is descriptive: contrivance was most likely at work. Otherwise, if the result is eccentric but startlingly successful – often metaphoric – it might be ascribed to inspiration. This is so even if the poet can say, 'How obvious – why didn't I see that before?':

What respite from her thrilling toil
Did Beauty ever take?
But work might be electric rest
To those that magic make.

The two modifiers, "thrilling" and "electric" make the poetry of these lines. "Thrilling", a most unlikely companion of "toil", confers upon it a coat of many colours. "Electric", (reinforced by the repeated short *e* in "rest") turns on a powerful switch so that "rest" all but sizzles. The inspired choice of a word is made with open eyes that see what is right there, but such seeing does not happen at will.

Open-eyed, Dickinson didn't so much use metaphors to illuminate her poems as make poems from metaphors. Her very thinking was so shaped by imagery that it seems to have been metaphoric to begin with. That she reduced vast themes to little stanzas might be a metaphor for her talent for compacting, and sometimes also for her domesticating experience, putting nature, eternity – almost anything – in terms of housekeeping and the homely. This is redeemed from any belittling of her subjects by an astonishing sheer rightness of imagery – by what she made physical through language.

There are many poems that seem to be for Sue, some expressing love, others referring sadly to their estrangement. One, 'Success is counted sweetest', quoted in the Introduction, was sent meaningfully to her. Still another of these is a prolonged metaphor: Scornful, bitter, and brilliant, it begins "It dropped so low in my regard/ I heard it hit the ground", and ends with Dickinson denouncing herself "For entertaining plated wares/ Upon my silver shelf". This poem with its parlour imagery shows how smoothly and cleverly she could write.

We find personification everywhere in her poems, either developed or casually implied, things quickened into personhood through her warmly assumed kinship with all. The inert *it* becomes *he*, and in the case of nature, *she*. Even "News" is alive: "How News must feel when travelling/ If News have any heart". Perhaps it was Wadsworth in San Francisco she was trying to conjure up in her graphic city poem, 'I could die to know', with its muscle-men image, "Houses hunch the house/ With their brick shoulders".

Nature can be a housewife wielding a many-coloured broom at sunset. Or, similarly, "Like brooms of steel/ The snow and wind/ Had swept the winter street", where you feel snow and wind scouring your face like steel bristles, and see the metallic sheen of ice bared underfoot – all in those few words. Nature may also be a cook "in an opal apron,/ Mixing fresher air" after a storm; a pretty personification wearing the rainbows that hang in the misted air before it clears.

Emily Dickinson, who knew her fabrics, applied them to her observations, with "Broadcloth hearts are firmer/ Than those of organdy"; misery making "Midnight's awful pattern/ In the goods of day"; and this superb summing up, "My moment of brocade". Clothing fits in here, too: " ... the Daffodil/ Unties her yellow bonnet".

Her same right-seeing puts a red squirrel's teeth in a kitchen: "His cutlery he keeps/ Within his russet lips". The parlour clock contains the running of quick, little feet besides the slow *tock-tock* of a walking horse: "We were listening to the seconds races/ And the hoofs of the clock".

Further afield, the child behind her eyes embodies landscape: With an intent attitude, "The Hills erect their purple heads,/ The Rivers lean to see". Everything within a self can combine with what is indoors and out; there are no boundaries.

She could also turn domesticity on its head:

> The grave my little cottage is,
> Where keeping house for thee
> I make my parlor orderly
> And lay the marble tea.

Cosy has gone creepy – a warm tea setting turns shockingly cold and hard thanks to the adjectival "marble". Compare it with the thawing out in this triplet, written upon the death of Higginson's two-month-old daughter:

> A dimple in the tomb
> Makes that ferocious room
> A home.

Although the dimple, summing up happy, tender beauty, has been savaged in all its vulnerability by "that ferocious room" (a metaphor that beggars interpretation), the life that was – because it was and because we loved it – for a moment can tame even the concept of death.

There are whole poems deserving regard with no end other than description. Dickinson was fascinated by storms, and some of these images are strokes of a child's crayon drawings put into words: "The lightning showed a yellow beak/ And then a livid claw"; and at the dining room table, "The lightning is a yellow fork/ From tables in the sky/ By inadvertent fingers dropped".

Here, a lightning simile's three nouns ("flash", "click", and "suddenness") imitate revelation:

> The soul's distinct connection
> With immortality
> Is best disclosed by danger
> Or quick calamity,
>
> As lightning on a landscape
> Exhibits sheets of place
> Not yet suspected but for flash
> And click and suddenness.

"Sheets of place" conveys by its pun on the word "sheets" the flat, bleached look that lightning gives to voluminous and colourful space.

Always sensitive to atmosphere and temperature, she recreated the green light that heralds a rainstorm:

> There came a wind like a bugle.
> It quivered through the grass,
> And a green chill upon the heat
> So ominous did pass.
> We barred the windows and the doors
> As from an emerald ghost ...

Eleven years earlier, she caught the rain's sometimes scary arrival from the distance with the phrase, "A coming as of hosts". The later line in that poem, "It warbled in the road", gives accurate and musical voice to that rain's runoff after a storm. After rain (from a letter): "The Road is full of little Mirrors".

As one who always remembered her manners, she would have liked to play hostess in her wind poem to the "rapid, footless guest", who had "tapped like a tired man" before inviting himself in through the opened door, flitted around the room unable to sit down, then flurriedly tapped again when ready to leave. With the wind's speech compared to " ... the push/ Of numerous humming birds" (note the *m*'s), she brought perfectly to life the sounds, and made visible a strong draft of air in, "His countenance a billow". And again more sounds, the breathy chromatics, just right:

> His fingers, as he passed
> Let go a music as of tunes
> Blown tremulous in glass.

In a sinister, sibilant poem, frost for her became another visitor:

> Who influences flowers
> Till they are orderly as busts
> And elegant as glass,
>
> Who visits in the night,
> And, just before the sun,
> Concludes his glistening interview,
> Caresses, and is gone.

Besides the *s*'s, note the repetition of *l* and *g* and *gl* and *cl* that create further glassification by association of sound. In another frost poem where dew "stiffens quietly to quartz", the verb "stiffen" adds rigor mortis to the drop turned into "quartz", strengthened by the added *qu* of quietly.

She played with effects, too. The poem, 'The name of it is Autumn', a curiosity, shows Dickinson's macabre side exercising itself by making a rather horrid colour picture of autumn out of blood. It is as if she stuffed the quatrains with all the words to bloody it that she could – arteries, veins, globules, stain, scarlet, ruddy, rose, and vermillion – to get intense red. And in the lovely but violent "Split the lark and you'll find the music,/ Bulb after bulb in silver rolled", seven *l*-sounds combine in a smooth vowel progression – one of her few sustained examples of matching sound and sense – making quicksilvery balls palpable.

The dandelion gone to seed – a rank pest to most – receives fine treatment in the tiny poem: "Its little ether hood/ Doth sit upon its head":

Till when it slips away
A nothing at a time,
And dandelion's drama
Expires in a stem.

Thanks to Dickinson's loving scrutiny of this one plant, we may be equally enchanted by other individuals in the vegetable kingdom.

Dickinson reproduced something of her delight in the brilliant, nigh-invisible hummingbird with two poems, 17 years apart. The first begins:

Within my garden rides a bird
Upon a single wheel
Whose spokes a dizzy music make
As 'twere a travelling mill.

Then, when "his fairy gig/ Reels in remoter atmospheres", she and her dog wonder if this was imagined:

But he, the best logician,
Refers my clumsy eye
To just vibrating blossoms:
An exquisite reply!

This is an instance of her lightest touch.

The second poem handles this subject differently, concentrating on colour, speed, and weight:

A route of evanescence
With a revolving wheel,
A resonance of emerald,
A rush of cochineal,
And every blossom on the bush
Adjusts its tumbled head ...

By contrast, when Dickinson wrote about water, she used spare language to step beyond reflection and stare into its mystery. It is fitting that she speaks in words as clear as water itself, telling us that we do not see with the proper simplicity but through eyes clouded by ideas, and that the commonest ingredient we deal with is one of the strangest:

> What mystery pervades a well!
> The water lives so far –
> A neighbor from another world
> Residing in a jar
>
> Whose limit none have ever seen,
> But just his lid of glass,
> Like looking every time you please
> In an abyss's face.

Strangeness, the stuff of art, was an unfathomable well of renewal for Dickinson as a poet and as a person. 'But nature is a stranger yet', and the poem ends:

> To pity those that know her not
> Is helped by the regret
> That those who know her, know her less
> The nearer her they get.

Going from well-water to the ocean, while its surface may imitate human attributes, below it seethes in vast menace. A highly unusual metaphor presents it as a boisterous bully at play:

> Three times the billows threw me up,
> Then caught me like a ball,
> Then made blue faces in my face ...

This comes from the middle of a poem about a dark night of the soul that begins "Three times we parted, Breath and I", and ends with the exultant "Then sunrise kissed my chrysalis/ And I stood up – and lived!". All aspects of the sea are personified, besides Breath, the Winds, and Sunrise.

The originality of the three lines quoted, and the excellence of many other excerpts, reinforce the argument for reading Dickinson's work whole. This poem wouldn't occur in a selection, not being quite resolved. (For instance, how does the chrysalis fit in with the sea?)

Here is an undated poem that invokes a scene without using any description. Through a statement delivered casually, then pared further down, a space grows ever larger behind the thinned-out words:

To make a prairie it takes clover and one bee,
One clover and a bee,
And revery.
The revery alone will do
If bees are few.

Made out of next-to-nothing, remarkably it leaves you in meadowy vastness.

3

Poems

People have very strong and certain views about Emily Dickinson's poems, even when the certainty doesn't always seem justified. And though they complain loudly about her faults, they conclude by acknowledging her poetic power, and that she is one of the greatest poets of all. Sometimes this is on the strength of a mere handful of poems, but few would agree on which handful. (This should reassure some of us.) It also shows what a unique quality Dickinson has – that she could be so controversial and irritating, and still emerge as a supreme poet.

Included here is a question about how much we ought to criticise poems never edited for official publication. We know about her habits of revision, and that hardly anything was final. This works to her advantage – we are largely forced to take her as she comes. Besides, she has a waif's appeal: While with other poets the rhetoric, perfect rhymes, and regular rhythms fill in where poetry flags, Dickinson's lapses in inspiration go without crutches, and it is almost churlish of us to point these out. We may be persuaded to treat her poems kindly even if in exasperation. Furthermore, if we patronise them, they rise up instantly in formidable power and put us in our place.

So that is one unorthodox aspect of her unorthodox poems. Our discussions of them tend to be on her terms.

Another – her hallmark – is somewhat unusual. Due to Dickinson's poems being compressed, they yield experiences that are deep and single rather than multiple – implosions rather than explosions, and immediate rather than arrived at through luxurious echoes, rhythms, and thickets of words.

As mentioned by the British poet James Reeves, each poem is best seen in the context of the entire collection. While Dickinson's best poems come as many small parcels, some of her best poetry and description come as parts of other parcels. Furthermore, the poems work off each other in recurring themes, with everything loosely woven together by voice and personality. Deciding which poem to discuss regrettably means disregarding others equally good.

Since unevenness is a Dickinson trait to expect, we must look out for lines, images, and passages within poems that don't necessarily live up to them. A number of poems have firecracker starts not followed by that initial drive. 'Water is taught by thirst' was noted earlier. After another, 'They shut me up in prose', the poem sags into an altered meaning. And next, 'Who has not found the heaven below/ Will fail of it above' needs only silence in which to contemplate this, beautifully put; the added lines seem merely to fill out a quatrain.

Here, while the show-stopping first line is a poem in itself, what follows piles up detail and color until we half-discern garden scenes of other days:

> This quiet dust was gentlemen and ladies,
> And lads and girls –
> Was laughter and ability and sighing,
> And frocks and curls.
>
> This passive place a summer's nimble mansion
> Where bloom and bees
> Exist, an oriental circuit,
> Then cease, like these.

The "passive place" would be with vegetation dead and matted down, either just before winter or spring. "Mansion" may require a pause to visualise the billowing structures of a green-leaf-roofed garden, whose "nimble" makes it lively with breezes and bugs. "Oriental" brings to the summery cycle a swarm of colours and textures identified with the Far East's bazaars.

The tale, that 'flesh is grass' and that grass is grass, is told in iambic pentameter alternated with iambic dimeter lines rhymed perfectly. They fit the sense every time – the long lines for expansion, the short achieving drama at the end.

A great many poems come under the heading of love with its various distinctions, such as friendship, admiration, sympathy, and grieving a loss. Some – we often have to guess which ones – had Sue in mind, some we know were for Samuel Bowles, a few perhaps for Jesus Christ, and others for unnamed persons. Those to do with love of an unattainable man stand out as such, leading to urgent poems about separation; about starvation or thirst as metaphors for her terrible privation; poems protesting fidelity to secret wifehood; and those looking forward to triumph after death, when she and her lover could finally be together. As with the 'Master' letters, the openness of these love poems makes us uncomfortable as though we were somewhat snooping. Harrowing, they leave us sad and in awe of her poetry after we put them down. The real triumph at which Dickinson eventually arrived was more than survival after missing out on love. She emerged from an agonised time with some knowledge of that state of living bliss sought after by meditators and mystics, having discovered it through an active will to live in the face of despair.

This is one of her most severe and telling poems:

> The hallowing of pain
> Like hallowing of heaven,
> Obtains at a corporeal cost.
> The summit is not given
>
> To him who strives severe
> At middle of the hill,
> But he who has achieved the top –
> All is the price of all.

Her extreme pain became something holy to her, no less so than the thought of heaven, having been needed to arrive later at the fullness of living. She spelled this out with no softening. The last line, if not the whole poem, should be kept in memory for when we need it.

The form here, short metre, 3-3-4-3, was used so often by her that it became second poetic nature and could communicate anything, as did common metre. The second and fourth lines rhyme only half-way, but we don't need more. If we wonder about the grammatical use of *he*, stanza two, line three, it is better poetically than grammatically, and can be made right if we understand 'finds' before the last line.

Because of her religious background, Dickinson often used Christian imagery. Being crowned implied heavenly status or suggested a crown of thorns. "Calvary" stood for her own suffering, sacred because her love for a man was joined with the excruciating. (At times this fits, at other times it seems somewhat formulaic.) In 'Title divine is mine –/ The wife without the sign', she summed up her situation in the lines, "Born – bridalled – shrouded/ In a day". Falling in love, committing to it, and realising that this was all there was for her had occurred simultaneously. The poem could apply aptly to the man of God, Charles Wadsworth – or even possibly to God Himself. J.V. Cunningham proposed that she still yearned for the conversion that failed in school, and that the Christian imagery might sometimes be understood within that context. Certain Calvinists believed that someone could choose to be of the elect without conversion, and it is not altogether out of the question that Dickinson wanted to consider herself married to Christ.

This, about a man, concludes that satisfaction could kill:

It might be lonelier
Without the loneliness.
I'm so accustomed to my fate,
Perhaps the other peace

Would interrupt the dark
And crowd the little room
Too scant by cubits to contain
The sacrament of him.

I am not used to hope:
It might intrude upon,
Its sweet parade blaspheme the place
Ordained to suffering.

It might be easier
To fail with land in sight,
Than gain my blue peninsula
To perish of delight.

Loneliness existing as a concept that others can share gives comfort, and the pangs of actual loneliness, unexpressed, would be worse without it. By now Dickinson is so used to her state that peace and hope with its "sweet parade" would be out of place and disrespectful of suffering, which deserves supremacy. Notice the scriptural imagery – the words "sacrament", "blaspheme", and "cubits" (a measurement from the Bible). Dickinson has stated variously that fulfilment could be deadly, such as in 'As if I asked a common alms', where seeing dawn would shatter her with its beauty. Other examples can be found in the poems about starvation and thirst.

The form is, again, 3-3-4-3, and the only real rhyming of second and fourth lines occurs in the last stanza, being ignored or partial in the other stanzas.

Dickinson's independence and fortitude nowhere showed more proudly than in the stand she took against disappointment – staring it down, controlling it with attitude. From a time and place not far from Amherst came this advice on how to behave well: "Win as though you were used to it, lose as though you liked it." (Isabella Stewart Gardner, eminent Boston patron of art, 1840 – 1924.) Dickinson renounced what the love relationship would have given her to keep destiny from having the last word. One way she did this was to tell herself that deprivation is superior to fulfilment, in which appreciation gets lost. Aggressively she chose to prefer it, because wanting gives things their true worth. Even so, as she struggled hard with this, using food and drink imagery, she knew all the while that renunciation, "a piercing virtue, ... is the choosing/ Against itself", and that this noblest means of handling her deprivation had mutilated her.

Whereas most of Dickinson's love poems show her stricken feelings, here are several fragments of wonderful tenderness (and poetry) extracted from otherwise ordinary poems. 'Forever at his side to walk' was written after some correspondence with Wadsworth and his first visit to her in Amherst. She lets herself imagine how it might be – "Two lives – one being now" – and tells straight out through food imagery how she yearns to give:

> Forever of his fate to taste –
> If grief, the largest part,

If joy, to put my piece away
For that beloved heart

Where such awesome poetry is concerned, it doesn't matter whether what happened in the following was real or fantasised. Again we have sea imagery:

He touched me, so I live to know
That such a day, permitted so,
I groped upon his breast.

It was a boundless place to me
And silenced, as the awful sea
Puts minor streams to rest.

By the early 1800s "awful" was used pretty much as in the early 2000s, but Dickinson would have meant 'awe-inspiring' here, with overtones of 'exceedingly great' (an intensive).

Next, in 'The spry arms of the wind' with its lovely image at the end, written when Wadsworth was living in San Francisco, she describes travelling to her beloved's far-off town in the arms of the wind. It can wait for her while she goes on her errand:

To ascertain the house
And is the soul at home,
And hold the wick of mine to it
To light, and then return.

Closing the sequences in her most important experience are two extracts using the same image. This one was written close to the time Wadsworth returned to Philadelphia:

The smouldering embers blush!
Oh heart within the coal,
Hast thou survived so many years?
The smouldering embers smile!

And showing the same emotional temperature in 'Long years apart can make no/ Breach a second cannot fill', when Dickinson was thought to be corresponding with him again:

The embers of a thousand years
Uncovered by the hand
That fondled them when they were fire
Will stir and understand.

Four years later he was to pay her a final visit, knowing that he was going to die soon.

This tightly-wrought poem has been much anthologised, its last line weighted in its simplicity like no other:

The soul selects her own society,
Then shuts the door.
To her divine majority
Present no more.

Unmoved, she notes the chariots pausing
At her low gate;
Unmoved, an emperor be kneeling
Upon her mat.

I've known her from an ample nation
Choose one,
Then close the valves of her attention
Like stone.

Whether about friendship or, more likely, love (see also "Of all the souls that stand create/ I have elected one ..."), makes no difference, since both can seem absolute.

The phrase "divine majority" implies a Royal We, a walloping importance for the self and its chosen one. Being together lifts the separateness of each out of the category of minorities into the realm of a majority, imposing in size through the embedded 'maior', Latin for 'greater', 'larger', 'more grand'. Furthermore, this new state bestows divinity – not literally godliness, but an emotional sense of being blessed in its ardent union beyond being impressed by, or even aware of, the prestige and titles of those who yearn to be included. (In another interpretation, an implied comma after "to her" would indicate that what presents itself, even though it be a gathering of gods, is beneath notice.) Rank and wealth are irrelevant to love. Throughout, the soul insists on being without pretension, simple as a "low gate" and a "mat". If one thinks of the physical heart, "valves" are soft, moving, and organic; and when they change to stone, the choice is that much more conclusive.

The ending is one of Dickinson's strongest. (Perhaps the only other comparable comes at the end of 'No rack can torture me', and hits hard: "Captivity is consciousness,/ So's liberty.")

The four-beat lines with feminine endings (final syllable unstressed) alternate with two-beat lines whose rhymes are masculine (final syllable stressed) and exact only in the first stanza, although "one" and "stone" are eye-rhymes. The first line of the first stanza has five beats only if we make the *y* in society into an unnaturally emphasised *ee*. After reading the poem through once, we find a reason to standardise the feel of four beats in the longer lines by hurrying "society" to shorten it, and lingering upon "majority" to lengthen it. The form fits the text most successfully. One could imagine Dickinson building backwards from the last line whose two beats perfectly frame "like stone", slowed to one stress per word. We are prepared by the line, "choose one", equally deliberate and slow but abstract, giving the word "stone" full weight when it drops at the end.

Dickinson's most troubled poems were composed between 1862 and 1864 when she went through emotional storms that threatened her balance. The second and third 'Master' letters had been drafted, and the terror she wrote to Higginson about may have been that she felt she was going mad. Those who have known the ferocity of despair can tell that she did not exaggerate. Without the experience to reflect, no one could or would want to write these poems. By themselves they could be discussed at book-length. Quite apart from their value as poetry, they serve to assure others that they, too, can win through. Her giving voice to such ordeals, as have few other poets, is one reason why her poems have such profound appeal. As for her having been called Amherst's Madame de Sade by Camille Paglia, this epithet is inaccurate, her tortures being masochistic. She had survived childhood with the inner savage intact, able to rejoice in being alive. Her suffering turned this against herself.

While there is no evidence that Dickinson had bouts of insanity, she certainly had a glimpse into its abyss. Surreal, yet accurately observed, this poem is among the most horrendous in English:

I felt a funeral in my brain,
And mourners to and fro
Kept treading, treading, till it seemed
That sense was breaking through.

And when they all were seated,
A service like a drum
Kept beating, beating, till I thought
My mind was going numb.

And then I heard them lift a box
And creak across my soul
With those same boots of lead again,
Then space began to toll,

As all the heavens were a bell,
And being but an ear,
And I and silence some strange race
Wrecked solitary here.

And then a plank in reason broke,
And I dropped down and down
And hit a world at every plunge,
And finished knowing then.

What inspired the poem could have been a state produced by the deepest despair over either losing her chance to love, or to be united with God. Here we have utterly original poetry – not this time from language, but from Dickinson's describing a funeral that possesses her. It emanates from her own heartbeat, whose rhythm keeps recurring from the beginning through to the end's erratic plunge from reason, striking worlds on the way down. These heartbeat images are the mourners' treading ("sense was breaking through" means that it was broken through); the service beating like a drum; the boots of the pallbearers creaking in unison; the tolling bell; and, finally, in the breakdown of reason, the thumps of the self's buffetings in its freefall down towards a disintegrated state. "Finished knowing" could either be a blackout, or the falling into a mental pit beyond thought where there seems no way out.

Common metre works naturally and effectively here, but some padding should be pointed out: The last two lines in stanza four bring extraneous images into an otherwise amazing poem.

Kindred in subject but without the hypnotic strangeness is 'I felt a cleaving in my mind', a visually clear, tactile picture of a schizophrenic episode. Thought becomes disconnected, and "Sequence ravelled out of sound/ Like balls upon a floor" – a picture of confusion that you can see and hear.

The best and most focused part begins this poem of pure nightmare (not completed with the same intensity). As always, Dickinson's subject not being made explicit makes the poem apply much more broadly:

> 'Twas like a maelstrom with a notch
> That nearer every day
> Kept narrowing its boiling wheel,
> Until the agony
>
> Toyed coolly with the final inch
> Of your delirious hem …

The poem ends, "Which anguish was the utterest then,/ To perish or to live?"

When the fury of an ordeal has subsided, a person emerges static from trauma, not yet fully alive:

> After great pain, a formal feeling comes.
> The nerves sit ceremonious, like tombs.
> The stiff heart questions, 'Was it He that bore?'
> And, 'Yesterday, or centuries before?'
>
> The feet, mechanical, go round
> A wooden way
> Of ground or air or ought,
> Regardless grown,
> A quartz contentment like a stone.
>
> This is the hour of lead
> Remembered, if outlived,
> As freezing persons recollect the snow –
> First chill – then stupor – then the letting go.

Inert, the nerves are now like stone effigies of themselves on tombs of former feelings. The heart is stiff from its long-endured emotions, and also stiff as though dead. In the third line, Dickinson was referring to Christ, wondering if it had been He, not she herself, who had undergone the agony, such had been its magnitude. She has lost all sense of time and, numbed, goes through daily living by rote. "A quartz contentment" means that even relief at having survived feels stony, though white and bright because she is purged. Memory of this ice-cold "hour of lead", if it is survived, will always stop at the point of slipping towards madness. (In the poem, 'It was not death, for I stood up', she wrote of despair that was like "chaos – stopless – cool", another picture of the state described earlier.)

See how Dickinson broke up the lines in stanza two to avoid rhyming round/ground. This makes "A wooden way", all by itself, apply both before and after, and "regardless grown", falling alone, go with either "ground", "air", and "ought", or "contentment". The poem starts off in iambic pentameter, rhyming *aabb*, then the pattern of verse and rhyme breaks up until re-established in the last two lines.

Throughout Dickinson's life, the dominance of religion and the unceasing deaths around her kept the subject of mortality very much to the fore. In eight taut, dynamic lines, Dickinson has celebrated a universal situation that needed saying:

> That short potential stir
> That each can make but once –
> That bustle so illustrious
> 'Tis almost consequence –
>
> Is the *éclat* of death.
> Oh, thou unknown renown
> That not a beggar would accept
> Had he the power to spurn!

If someone didn't get his 15 minutes of fame during life, he gets it when he is dead. This is the one time when persons are unfailingly treated with concern and respect, and when only good is broadcast about them – yet not even the most miserable of us would want it. The poetry here is the hardest to explain, the pleasure given by the language being especially subtle. "Short" modifying "stir" is effective because the repeated *s*, *r*, and *t* fortify each other in their Anglo-Saxon strength, creating an energetic burst undiminished by the Latinate "potential" that separates them with its suave sound and reminds us that we are still alive, still able to anticipate. The poignancy is that our guaranteed moment of fame, so concentrated that it almost amounts to importance, occurs only once (just as we have died) – a "consequence" deftly and most cruelly undercut by "almost". The word "consequence", taken apart, means 'with something to follow', and implies leaving ripples in the wake (pun intended) of the event. But all it amounts to is mere fuss and bustle no matter how expensive, elaborate, and impressive. (Notice the three *us* sounds repeated in "illustrious" and "bustle" – they actually rustle.)

"*Éclat*", here connected with death, is what makes the poem poetry, a word for an explosion of brilliance and sound and splendour, a spot-lighting of life itself. Exactly what your "renown" will be after you die is still unknown, permitting scope for fantasising. All this occurs yet again in the 3-3-4-3 form, as always remarkable for what Dickinson puts into it. The half-rhymes are adequate.

Her death-watch poem proves what extraordinary poetry can come from ordinary words:

> The last night that she lived,
> It was a common night
> Except the dying – this to us
> Made nature different.
>
> We noticed smallest things,
> Things overlooked before,
> By this great light upon our minds
> Italicized, as 'twere.
>
> As we went out and in
> Between her final room
> And rooms where those to be alive
> Tomorrow were a blame
>
> That others could exist
> While she must finish quite,
> A jealousy for her arose
> So nearly infinite.

We waited while she passed;
It was a narrow time.
Too jostled were our souls to speak.
At length the notice came.

She mentioned, and forgot;
Then lightly as a reed
Bent to the water, struggled scarce,
Consented, and was dead.

And we, we placed the hair
And drew the head erect;
And then an awful leisure was
Belief to regulate.

While the scene is illuminated with mystery and meaning by "this great light upon our minds", the word "italicized" says it afresh and makes the poetry twice over. "Final" used with "room" is smoother in sound than "last" would be, and has a funerary hue from the Latin.

Then two hardly admissible states of mind are declared: rage against friends for being alive when she was dying; and jealousy – wanting to be the one closest to her, thought of by her at this moment. "Narrow time" is the focus that is squeezed into depth brought about by the occasion, everyone dear to the dying woman being together in rooms as well as in the sorrow. "Too jostled" means upset and either weeping or restraining tears, as well as busy interacting. This is an example of how poetry can cover multiplicity, which touches on a third image, that of a channel introduced by "narrow" and "jostled", not revealed until the next stanza where it has been saved for the dying.

Here death is not the sea, but stream-water. After a few, half-conscious words ("mentioned" is just right for her abstracted, broken-off phrase), the woman is pulled away in the current of time like a reed bending to water, a stream whose sides had narrowed for the force of this passage, jostling all in its flow as it bears away her life. The end stanza returns to the room and the friends whose last service is to straighten her, the way water had aligned the reed with its current.

In the second-to-last line, the friction of "awful" against "leisure", describing the mourning period, brings about poetry through incongruity. Here, "awful" differs from the same word in "the awful sea", from the poem, 'He touched me, so I live to know'. In this instance, it means a time still reverberating with awe of death, and also (although Dickinson might not have intended this) exceedingly hard to take.

It is a pity about the inversion in the last line, especially as Dickinson got no rhyme from this. She may have rightly considered "regulate" a better match in sound for "erect" than "belief". Yet there are no exact rhymes in the poem. Anyway, she wisely didn't force the language, keeping half-rhymes where they fit naturally throughout the smooth, familiar 3-3-4-3-beat stanza form.

Note the impersonal "the" instead of 'her' before "hair" and "head" in the last stanza. The American critic, Yvor Winters, pointed out how Dickinson emphasised the division between the living and the dead. One way was to refer to the corpse as "it". An example: 'If I may have it when it's dead/ I'll be contented so', a poem shocking and dreadful with pain, in which she looks forward to finally being allowed to spend a moment with her lover before his burial. Another instance: ''Twas warm at first, like us', in which the dead body is made horribly impersonal by coldness, weight, and the use of *it* in "'Twas".

Here is a poem in short metre written two years before Dickinson died, again a death watch:

> Still own thee, still thou art
> What surgeons call alive,
> Though slipping, slipping, I perceive
> To thy reportless grave.
>
> Which question shall I clutch?
> What answer wrest from thee
> Before thou dost exude away
> In the recallless sea?

Quiet, but central to the poetry, the word "exude" is more subtle than the watery ebbing or oozing to be expected with "sea". Rather than red blood gradually diluted when lapped into the green sea, this substance of person and personality is atomised through a slow, luminous transference of essence into the spirit medium beyond – an inexorable movement going one way only. The word "recallless", one of Dickinson's creations, has more pathos and point than would "irrevocable". "Call", embedded within, is a cry stopped dead before the annihilating sea that goes on forever.

This eternity poem, widely known, dates from 1859 – the year after Dickinson suddenly began to write poetry in earnest. The two stanzas give different views of our situation as mortals:

> Safe in their alabaster chambers,
> Untouched by morning
> And untouched by noon,
> Sleep the meek members of the resurrection –
> Rafter of satin and roof of stone.
>
> Grand go the years
> In the crescent above them,
> Worlds scoop their arcs
> And firmaments row,
> Diadems drop
> And Doges surrender
> Soundless as dots
> On a disc of snow.

Originally there were babbling bees and sweet birds in the second stanza, and her sister-in-law, Sue, complained. She complained about this version also, saying in a letter that it did not go with "the ghostly shimmer" of the first stanza, and lamented that Emily had never made a peer for it – that probably "her kingdom didn't hold one".

The first stanza is white and closed, close-up if not claustrophobic, with life-sized figures lying dead in timeless silence. (In fact, there is a silence to the whole poem.) The word "meek" – everyone acquiescing to death – suggests the slight forward bend to the neck as the skull rests upon a pillow. It also tells something about how these people had lived their lives as good citizens and Christians, doing what was expected of them and bowing to the will of God in order to qualify for heaven. Is there irony here in this word "meek" – that these people lived according to the belief that they would be 'saved', and here their frightful bones lie, shut tight – safe – in satin-lined coffins? That now they are oblivious not only of any paradise but even of the beautiful phases of each passing day – perhaps the nearest to heaven that they had ever come? Perhaps Dickinson was trying out the concept.

In the second stanza, we zoom from that close-up to heavenly bodies moving telescopically far away in arcs. Note the "crescent" shape of orbits and of the sky (all we can see from our positions upon the globe of earth) repeated in "arcs", and in the acts of "scooping" and of "rowing". Then, just as suddenly, from the perspective of planets and stars we view our tiny historical turbulence – of monarchies, and of glorious Venice (implied by "Doges" who ruled that city, their Latinate title being allied to 'duke', and *duce* – 'leader' in Italian; Mussolini was called *Il Duce*). The dead lie under these cycles of human history as well as the revolving heavens. All that mattered and that once triumphed is now gone, reduced to dots like snowflakes (again the white and cold) disappearing in silence into the disc of wintry earth (arc shape repeated) now no bigger than a thumb-nail.

If you read the poem out loud, you notice the underlying pattern. In stanza one, the first line has four stresses. Lines two and three together make a five-stress line, which matches line four. Line five has four stresses to match line one. Only the second line begins with an iambic foot, and the rest with trochees, although it is simpler to measure this poem by stresses rather than feet, the rhythm being rather irregular. (See how *r* followed by *s* is repeated in that last line, drawing the image together through an effect of aphorism.)

Stanza two, with two stresses per line, might also be a four-line stanza with all the four-stress lines broken in half. From the beginning, trochees start off every other line. (The *d*'s in the last four lines are repeated to create again a kind of aphorism.)

In stanza one, notice how "chambers" and "resurrection" end lines with weak syllables; likewise in stanza two, "above them" and "surrender". This gives a rhythmic swing and smoothness to the lines that would otherwise be somewhat choppy. They even suggest more rhyme than there actually is, with "noon" and "stone" rhyming roughly in the first stanza, and "row" and "snow" in the second.

One could connect the encumbered, irregular music of the first stanza with heavy earth and stone. The repetitive form in stanza two, with its quicker music and vertical structure, reflects the distant orbitings back and forth.

While this poem contains no inspired juxtapositions of language, stanza one is well described, and the contrasted perspectives make poetry of plight by means of the shifting focal points.

Those who wonder how Emily Dickinson could know human nature so deeply when she spent her life at home need only think about her subject matter. One of her preoccupations was memory which she explored mostly as a Gothic-style hell of remorse. Another was consciousness or mind with the ambivalences of self in its many layers. The interior self, called a friend, could just as easily come alive with a horror-movie frisson as a spy. All this is subject matter that must be dug into alone. Courageous and sensitive, Dickinson always reported from within herself, which was the source of her power. In the same way she explored the topics of God, belief, heaven, and bliss – by saying how she found them.

From the year before she died, here is a final, bitter statement on God:

> Of God we ask one favor, that we may be forgiven –
> For what, he is presumed to know:
> The crime from us is hidden.
> Immured the whole of life
> Within a magic prison,
> We reprimand the happiness
> That too competes with heaven.

Not only do we ironically ask God to forgive us for crimes we cannot know, but we even have to denounce the happiness we have had because it competes with heaven – rather like condemning portraiture because it copies God in his creation of people. (In spite of this negative overview, Dickinson could at least say that her happiness did compete with heaven.)

While "Immured" bricks us up alive with its 'murus', Latin for wall, life as a magic prison dissolves into freedom by means of the Buddhist thinking – that life is illusion. The word "magic", airy and shifting with rainbow tints, lifts the cold, stone-grey prison into a fantasy: this is the core of the poetry here.

Listening carefully, we recognise the 3-3-4-3 pattern disguised by some rearranging in this preferred version, with two stanzas run together. There is no hard rhyming, but the whole poem is held together by the feminine half-rhymes – "forgiven", "hidden", "prison", "heaven" – occurring in alternate lines.

There is good reason to think that Dickinson had, like William Wordsworth, experiences associated with the spiritual life. When she wrote of awe, ecstasy, bliss, heaven, and of "The magic passive but extant/ That consecrated me", she was not being figurative; she lived with that. In a poem that begins, "One blessing had I than the rest/ So larger to my eyes", the blessing, never named, is "A perfect paralysing bliss" too large to measure – "a heaven below the heaven above – ", and she ends, "Why floods [of bliss] be served to us in bowls/ I speculate no more". In a letter she wrote, "To have lived is a bliss so powerful, we must die to adjust to it". Her garden was a cosmos where Dickinson found what had failed to come through official religion. She explained, in 'Some keep the Sabbath going to church', how she kept it with orchard and bobolink. The last two lines say what she repeated in many different ways: "So instead of getting to heaven at last,/ I'm going all along."

Undoubtedly, the insights that she achieved through persistent honesty, and that she put into poetry, helped Dickinson keep her balance and gave her inducement to live. She took pride in finding so much to engage her, stating that her business was "circumference" – one of her most loaded, favourite words – to encompass as far and deep as she could reach.

4

Circumference and Conclusion

Emily Dickinson's father, who had worried greatly about her delicate constitution, who had made it clear that women should stay at home – and not publish – could hardly complain about her withdrawal, even though privately he must have once expected his womenfolk to lead the appropriate behind-the-scenes community organisations. This could not have been long considered for his wife, a semi-invalid since the move to the Homestead. Vinnie, vigorously busy, seems not to have thought in that direction. Father had no hope of changing Emily, who once locked herself in the basement with a rocking chair when he had ordered her to go to church.

For Emily, constraints and privileges converged nicely with her needs. Between chores she could enjoy books and her passion for the natural world in a large garden and a conservatory ("Oh, honey of an hour"). And, in the solitary arena of her own room, where she had stood up to anguish and the threat of disintegration, she could write poem after poem undisturbed, often tiring herself out late at night to dull her "glittering retinue of nerves".

The breadth of living she enjoyed in her closeted world produced "circumference", by which she further meant regard for everything around her. She always experienced her life richly:

> The missing all prevented me
> From missing minor things.
> If nothing larger than a world's
> Departure from a hinge
> Or sun's extinction be observed,
> 'Twas not so large that I

Could lift my forehead from my work
For curiosity.

Because of this circumference there is something to be found for everyone in her immense trove of perceptions – from infinity to insects. (The poems about the spider, 'The spider holds a silver ball', and flies, 'Those cattle smaller than a bee', are delightful; and 'Further in summer than the birds' features katydids.) Those who enjoy Edgar Allen Poe and sci-fi will find, unexpectedly, poems for them, too. The same poet, who (in 'As children bid the guest "Good-Night"') likened flowers folding up at evening to children raising pretty lips to the guest, compared the split-second terror of death to:

> ... a face of steel
> That suddenly looks into ours
> With a metallic grin:
> The cordiality of Death
> Who drills his welcome in.

(From 'That after horror that 'twas us'.) In her variety she could range from the Victorian age to ours, all as part of herself.

That religious and social pressure didn't blinker her mind shows how much fundamental humanity there had been at home when she was growing up. Countering some of what was said about her stern, remote father, we have her letter of 1851 to Sue, telling of a preacher who put the congregation in nearly a frenzy by being perfectly ridiculous. Dickinson declared that she never heard her father so funny in mimicking him. "I know you'd have died laughing," she wrote. Vinnie's gift of mimicry had been inherited from him.

The circumference expressed by Dickinson was influenced by home, community, and something larger. She lived in a time when America was developing a golden age in literature and in painting. Emerson was encouraging a national literature for writers to speak their own truths, not those of classical Europe (and the same for artists of all disciplines); not what they were schooled in, but what they experienced. The capital secret was to convert life, not school-learning, into truth. Henry Wadsworth Longfellow, fostering a broad view, also cultivated self-definition. A translator of Dante's *Divine Comedy*, he was a force in bringing foreign literatures and languages to Harvard in order to nourish American identity. The excitement of the times would have refreshed theocratic and academic Amherst, which appreciated nature as a machine created by God.

Increasingly accessible by railroad, the American landscape's mountains, lakes, and rivers seemed the self-evident proof of divine origin looked for by the Calvinists. A viewer could be both thrilled by sublime scenery and challenged by its potential, nobody being too inhibited by a notion that making fortunes out of its resources, or simply by moving there, would destroy the sublimity. Even while Amherst grew, no housing developments were yet creeping up the other side of the wooded hills that Emily Dickinson saw from her window. Not having to consider this makes a difference to the depth of the very breath that one draws.

Those caught up in the era's Romanticism found the wild landscapes more picturesque and awesome than any ever dreamed of. Spectacular vistas that epitomised the Sublime – some not far from Massachusetts – were well known and glorified by the Hudson River School of painters. Meanwhile, in a landscape less grand, but no less stimulating to her, Dickinson watched the drama of rainstorms, blizzards, hoarfrost, moonlight, sunrises, and sunsets, with wildflowers and trees undergoing their seasons. It had and still has its character that is intense and spare, corresponding to the New Englanders. Robert Frost brought it to life in his poems. Emily Dickinson wrote about it often tinged with the Sublime in the domestic way she knew first-hand – Anti-Sublimity, if you will, but always communicating total involvement and awe. Two of her poems that go beyond depiction are 'There's a certain slant of light,/ Winter afternoons', and 'Presentiment is that long shadow on the lawn'. In summer no less than winter one can encounter the chill that enters the soul when the sun, going down, casts black shadows like coffins at one's feet.

The concept of Sublimity goes back to ancient cultures, to be found in the *Iliad*, the *Odyssey*, and the Bible. More recently we have *Paradise Lost*. Sublimity shows in the struggle to rise closer to the Divine through noble behaviour or through living according to spiritual values. In Dickinson's time it was chiefly looked for in theatrical landscapes with a gleam of the terrifying, as represented in literature and art. The more moving, the better, as its aim was transcendence.

The Transcendentalism connected with Emerson was more useful. It asserted the importance of the individual, and of living a spiritual life according to the good instincts of the common man. Think for yourself, act for yourself, and "Hitch your wagon to a star". Emerson was at his best in prose, in those memorable, epigrammatic sentences that rose to poetry.

While Dickinson and Emerson paralleled each other with inspired, homely image-making, we don't find her concerned with his Transcendentalism, and in fact, although she had read quite a few of his books, she didn't especially take note of him. This is surprising, but perhaps he was close to her in so many ways that she took him for granted.

A hungry reader who made unique use of what she read, Dickinson remained very much her own woman. It is not possible to catalogue her thoughts into anything like a philosophy; she didn't have formal doctrines to argue, and her insights were more reactions to what was at hand. Her personal force defines her, not a system of beliefs.

People who develop belief systems are at one remove from experience, theirs being the art of thought. Dickinson didn't draw back enough from what she wrote about to be concerned with art all that much, art being the *form* of expression. Hence the simplicity and, to some, the monotony of her verse forms. To her they sufficed.

If she sometimes slowed our access to her meanings by being knotty – compact and difficult to unravel – that sometimes unintentionally tied in with her idea that there is value in shielding a person from the shock of reality. We can digest only part of the "truth's superb surprise" at one time. Learning something should lead us indirectly to where we need to go without blinding us by excessive light or by rationality:

> Tell all the truth, but tell it slant –
> Success in circuit lies.
> Too bright for our inform delight,
> The truth's superb surprise.
> As lightning to the children eased
> With explanation kind,
> The truth must dazzle gradually
> Or every man be blind.

The thought in the line "Too much of proof affronts belief" (from 'So much of heaven has gone from earth') complements this.

Where not knotty, her poems are almost confrontations with their impact, their simple straight telling. Some of them have been termed definitional: 'The brain is wider than the sky'; 'A coffin is a small domain'; 'Dew is the freshet in the grass'; 'God is a distant, stately lover'.

Compared to other Victorian poets she was, along with Gerard Manley Hopkins and Walt Whitman, remarkably individual and modern, though she eschewed volubility for minimalism. *Direct* is the key word. She had much to say that was profound, and saying in her original way made it important poetry.

One wonders how Dickinson would feel about today's scholars labouring over her every trace. Would this be a validation of her private wars, or a violation? Although she seemed to know her worth as a poet, she was indeed private, having refused requests for poems to publish even after the death of her father. She had always approached Higginson as one seeking advice and guidance, yet she ignored his suggestions, knowing that she knew better. In time, confident enough of herself as a poet, she signed some of her letters with only her surname – something unheard of for women in those days.

Helen Hunt Jackson, a friend and highly successful writer, wrote to her in 1875 about her refusal to publish: "You are a great poet – and it is a wrong to the day you live in, that you will not sing aloud. When you are what men call dead, you will be sorry you were so stingy." Of Dickinson's 1,789 poems, only ten were published anonymously during her lifetime and most of these without her sanction.

One concept of proper publishing at the time was the circulation of literature among friends, and this was the one Dickinson embraced with something like six hundred poems. R.W. Franklin termed this "scribal publication", the handwritten poems sometimes being forwarded beyond their recipients. She may have renounced publishing in print in the same way she renounced love – to endure and handle not being able to have it. Such reticence would not only have pleased her father, but also allowed her to write the violent and otherwise strange poems without standardising her presentation. If she ever intended her work to find the public, others would have to cope with the mechanics.

It is because of Vinnie that Emily Dickinson's poems survived at all. Having been made to promise to destroy her sister's papers, Vinnie burned letters – which she later regretted – but then was astonished to discover a locked box that contained, on neatly-sewn packets, loose pages, and miscellaneous scraps of paper, an enormous collection of poems that nobody had known about. Unwilling to destroy these, and because they had not been clearly designated for burning, she turned them over to Sue to edit for publication.

Conceivably, Dickinson wrote her poems to stay fully alive, and as part of being alive, then considered letting them go when she died. If she truly meant Vinnie to burn everything, we can see her distinctly in relation to her poems – that they were an extension of that extraordinary woman who had understood so much beyond room and garden through a hard-won shining into her mind from another level of being. This was what mattered. Beyond, whatever contact she had wished to make through them with others was personal.

While Dickinson had once said that publishing was out of her element, unfitting to her "as Firmament to Fin" (as the sky to fish), she did mention elsewhere that "If fame belonged to me, I could not escape her". Conceivably too she let Vinnie choose whether or not to burn her manuscripts, leaving it up to the poems themselves whether or not they could inspire their way forward.

Sue, half-heartedly planning to print and circulate the poems but not publish them as a large venture, had accomplished little after two years, so Vinnie gave them to Mabel Todd.

She had never actually seen Dickinson, though she had several times been invited to stop by and sing at their piano. (Following her small recitals, Dickinson would send her down gifts such as a glass of sherry with a poem written during her singing.) While copying the manuscripts later, Todd grew more and more enthusiastic, and her assuring Higginson that she would do all the work persuaded him to help get them published. She typed up two hundred poems, and by 1890 a selection was ready. Eleven editions followed within the next two years, and a collection of Dickinson's letters that she edited was printed in 1893.

Higginson, besides helping with the eventual publication, had maintained a friendship with Dickinson that had been crucial to her.

She mentioned twice that he had saved her life, and he may well have done so by giving her an opening into the world that she needed and could manage. An influential and kindly man, he had been unable to evaluate poetry beyond its formal dress, but during the posthumous editing of Dickinson's work he developed new eyes, coming to an astounded appreciation of her poems that he had never had when she was alive, calling her a rare genius, a new star revealed.

With an early publication, a review for the *Atlantic Monthly* proclaimed that no other recent book could be as important to the literature of America. In the *New York Times*, Emily Dickinson was touted as being placed permanently and without doubt among the enduring poets of the English-speaking world; [and later] among the immortals. The *Saturday Review of Literature* praised her colossal substance. Louis Untermeyer, of the *American Mercury*, termed her the greatest woman poet of all time, possibly excepting Sappho. From Mark Van Doren in the *Nation*, she was much the best of women poets and came near the crown of all poetry. Today, after a period of crests and troughs with readers, her poems are still spreading into their rightful place, to be found in translation all over the world.

Her name jumps out from unexpected places. Aaron Copland's songs, 'Twelve Poems of Emily Dickinson', are performed and broadcast. In his tome on human nature, *The Blank Slate,* author Steven Pinker (also a linguist, and cognitive scientist at MIT) quoted her poem 'The brain is wider than the sky'. The notorious forger, Mark Hofmann, fooled (among others) experts at Sotheby's by imitating the thick strokes of her handwriting in a "newly found Dickinson poem" they listed in their 1997 catalogue. And in early 2003, Dickinson was one of three poets to be discussed in a White House literary symposium that had to be cancelled because of a strident intrusion of politics: one of the participants intended an anti-White-House demonstration. This would have been suited to Walt Whitman perhaps, but unseemly for Emily Dickinson – although she would stand forever as totally her private self in the middle of any ideological rumpus as she does in fame.

Meanwhile, her popularity keeps growing. Perhaps this has never shown more truly than when 'After great pain, a formal feeling comes' was widely posted and quoted following 11th September 2001. Those haunted by fire and death from Ground Zero turned to her words to speak for them. That is what a poet is for.

Select Bibliography

The Poems of Emily Dickinson, edited by R.W. Franklin (Belknap/ Harvard, 1998).
Text from the manuscripts of E.D., with original spelling, grammar, and punctuation.

Selected Poems of Emily Dickinson, edited and introduced by James Reeves (Heinemann, 1958). Text regularised as Dickinson might have done for publication, with classic introductory essay.

My Wars Are Laid Away in Books, by Alfred Habegger (Random House, 2001). Biography with conclusions based on most recent scholarship.

The Life of Emily Dickinson, by Richard B. Sewell (Harvard, 1974). Indispensable and exhaustive biography.

The Letters of Emily Dickinson, edited by Thomas H. Johnson (Harvard/Belknap, 1986). Expensive, but the complete Letters should be read with the poems.

Emily Dickinson – Bloom's Major Poets, edited by Harold Bloom (Chelsea House, 1999). A selection of extracts by leading critics.

Emily Dickinson – A Collection of Critical Essays, edited by Judith Farr (Prentice Hall, 1996). Range of essays introduced by Dickinson specialist.

Sexual Personae, by Camille Paglia ('Amherst's Madame de Sade') (Yale, 1990). Flamboyant presentation of Emily Dickinson's images of violence.

The Poet and the Murderer, by Simon Worrall (Dutton, 2002). Scrupulous uncovering of crimes including a forged Dickinson poem.

The Collected Essays of J.V. Cunningham, by J.V. Cunningham ('Sorting Out the Case of Dickinson') (Chicago: The Swallow Press, 1976). American writer discusses Dickinson for his own and our benefit.

Emily Dickinson: Three Views, by Archibald MacLeish, Louise Bogan, and Richard Wilbur (Amherst College Press, 1960). Three eminent poets on the poet.

Maule's Curse, by Yvor Winters ('Emily Dickinson and the Limits of Judgment') (New Directions, 1938). Well-known American critic speaks strongly.

GREENWICH EXCHANGE BOOKS

Greenwich Exchange Student Guides are critical studies of major or contemporary serious writers in English and selected European languages. The series is for the student, the teacher and 'common readers' and is an ideal resource for libraries. The *Times Educational Supplement* praised these books, saying, "The style of these guides has a pressure of meaning behind it. Students should learn from that ... If art is about selection, perception and taste, then this is it."

(ISBN prefix 1-871551- applies)
The series includes:
W.H. Auden by Stephen Wade (36-6)
Honoré de Balzac by Wendy Mercer (48-X)
William Blake by Peter Davies (27-7)
The Brontës by Peter Davies (24-2)
Robert Browning by John Lucas (59-5)
Samuel Taylor Coleridge by Andrew Keanie (64-1)
Joseph Conrad by Martin Seymour-Smith (18-8)
William Cowper by Michael Thorn (25-0)
Charles Dickens by Robert Giddings (26-9)
John Donne by Sean Haldane (23-4)
Ford Madox Ford by Anthony Fowles (63-3)
Thomas Hardy by Sean Haldane (35-1)
Seamus Heaney by Warren Hope (37-4)
Philip Larkin by Warren Hope (35-8)
Laughter in the Dark – The Plays of Joe Orton by Arthur Burke (56-0)
Philip Roth by Paul McDonald (72-2)
Shakespeare's Non-Dramatic Poetry by Martin Seymour-Smith (22-6)
Shakespeare's Othello by Matt Simpson (71-4)
Shakespeare's Sonnets by Martin Seymour-Smith (38-2)
Tobias Smollett by Robert Giddings (21-8)
Alfred, Lord Tennyson by Michael Thorn (20-X)
William Wordsworth by Andrew Keanie (57-9)

OTHER GREENWICH EXCHANGE BOOKS

Paperback unless otherwise stated.

Shakespeare's Sonnets
Martin Seymour-Smith
Martin Seymour-Smith's outstanding achievement lies in the field of literary biography and criticism. In 1963 he produced his comprehensive edition, in the old spelling, of *Shakespeare's Sonnets* (here revised and corrected by himself and Peter Davies in 1998). With its landmark introduction and its brilliant critical commentary on each sonnet, it was praised by William Empson and John Dover Wilson. Stephen Spender said of him "I greatly admire Martin Seymour-Smith for the independence of his views and the great interest of his mind"; and both Robert Graves and Anthony Burgess described him as the leading critic of his time. His exegesis of the *Sonnets* remains unsurpassed.
2001 • 194 pages • ISBN 1-871551-38-2

English Language Skills
Vera Hughes
If you want to be sure, (as a student, or in your business or personal life,) that your written English is correct, this book is for you. Vera Hughes' aim is to help you remember the basic rules of spelling, grammar and punctuation. 'Noun', 'verb', 'subject', 'object' and 'adjective' are the only technical terms used. The book teaches the clear, accurate English required by the business and office world. It coaches acceptable current usage and makes the rules easier to remember.
Vera Hughes was a civil servant and is a trainer and author of training manuals.
2002 • 142 pages • ISBN 1-871551-60-9

LITERARY CRITICISM

The Author, the Book and the Reader
Robert Giddings
This collection of essays analyses the effects of changing technology and the attendant commercial pressures on literary styles and subject matter. Authors covered include Charles Dickens, Tobias George Smollett, Mark Twain, Dr Johnson and John le Carré.
1991 • 220 pages • illustrated • ISBN 1-871551-01-3

Liar! Liar!: Jack Kerouac – Novelist
R.J. Ellis
The fullest study of Jack Kerouac's fiction to date. It is the first book to devote an individual chapter to every one of his novels. *On the Road, Visions of Cody* and *The Subterraneans* are reread in-depth, in a new and exciting way. *Visions of Gerard* and *Doctor Sax* are also strikingly reinterpreted, as are other daringly innovative writings, like 'The Railroad Earth' and his "try at a spontaneous *Finnegan's Wake*" – *Old Angel Midnight*. Neglected writings, such as *Tristessa* and *Big Sur*, are also analysed, alongside better-known novels such as *Dharma Bums* and *Desolation Angels*.
R.J. Ellis is Senior Lecturer in English at Nottingham Trent University.
1999 • 295 pages • ISBN 1-871551-53-6

BIOGRAPHY

The Good That We Do
John Lucas
John Lucas' book blends fiction, biography and social history in order to tell the story of his grandfather, Horace Kelly. Headteacher of a succession of elementary schools in impoverished areas of London, 'Hod' Kelly was also a keen cricketer, a devotee of the music hall, and included among his friends the great Trade Union leader, Ernest Bevin. In telling the story of his life, Lucas has provided a fascinating range of insights into the lives of ordinary Londoners from the First World War until the outbreak of the Second World War. Threaded throughout is an account of such people's hunger for education, and of the different ways government, church and educational officialdom ministered to that hunger. *The Good That We Do* is both a study of one man and of a period when England changed, drastically and forever.
John Lucas is Professor of English at Nottingham Trent University and is a poet and critic.
2001 • 214 pages • ISBN 1-871551-54-4

In Pursuit of Lewis Carroll
Raphael Shaberman
Sherlock Holmes and the author uncover new evidence in their investigations into the mysterious life and writing of Lewis Carroll. They examine published works by Carroll that have been overlooked by previous commentators. A newly discovered poem, almost certainly by Carroll, is published here.
Amongst many aspects of Carroll's highly complex personality, this book explores his relationship with his parents, numerous child friends, and the

formidable Mrs Liddell, mother of the immortal Alice. Raphael Shaberman was a founder member of the Lewis Carroll Society and a teacher of autistic children.

1994 • 118 pages • illustrated • ISBN 1-871551-13-7

Musical Offering
Yolanthe Leigh

In a series of vivid sketches, anecdotes and reflections, Yolanthe Leigh tells the story of her growing up in the Poland of the 30s and the Second World War. These are poignant episodes of a child's first encounters with both the enchantments and the cruelties of the world; and from a later time, stark memories of the brutality of the Nazi invasion, and the hardships of student life in Warsaw under the Occupation. But most of all this is a record of inward development; passages of remarkable intensity and simplicity describe the girl's response to religion, to music, and to her discovery of philosophy.

Yolanthe Leigh was formerly a Lecturer in Philosophy at Reading University.

2000 • 57 pages • ISBN: 1-871551-46-3

Norman Cameron
Warren Hope

Norman Cameron's poetry was admired by W.H. Auden, celebrated by Dylan Thomas and valued by Robert Graves. He was described by Martin Seymour-Smith as, "one of ... the most rewarding and pure poets of his generation ..." and is at last given a full-length biography. This eminently sociable man, who had periods of darkness and despair, wrote little poetry by comparison with others of his time, but always of a consistently high quality – imaginative and profound.

2000 • 221 pages • illustrated • ISBN 1-871551-05-6

POETRY

Adam's Thoughts in Winter
Warren Hope

Warren Hope's poems have appeared from time to time in a number of literary periodicals, pamphlets and anthologies on both sides of the Atlantic. They appeal to lovers of poetry everywhere. His poems are brief, clear, frequently lyrical, characterised by wit, but often distinguished by tenderness. The poems gathered in this first book-length collection counter the brutalising ethos of contemporary life, speaking of and for the virtues of modesty, honesty and gentleness in an individual, memorable way.

2000 • 47 pages • ISBN 1-871551-40-4

Baudelaire: Les Fleurs du Mal
Translated by F.W. Leakey
Selected poems from *Les Fleurs du Mal* are translated with parallel French texts and are designed to be read with pleasure by readers who have no French as well as those who are practised in the French language.
F.W. Leakey was Professor of French in the University of London. As a scholar, critic and teacher he specialised in the work of Baudelaire for 50 years and published a number of books on the poet.
2001 • 153 pages • ISBN 1-871551-10-2

Lines from the Stone Age
Sean Haldane
Reviewing Sean Haldane's 1992 volume *Desire in Belfast*, Robert Nye wrote in *The Times* that "Haldane can be sure of his place among the English poets." This place is not yet a conspicuous one, mainly because his early volumes appeared in Canada and because he has earned his living by other means than literature. Despite this, his poems have always had their circle of readers. The 60 previously unpublished poems of *Lines from the Stone Age* – "lines of longing, terror, pride, lust and pain" – may widen this circle.
2000 • 53 pages • ISBN 1-871551-39-0

Wilderness
Martin Seymour-Smith
This is Martin Seymour-Smith's first publication of his poetry for more than twenty years. This collection of 36 poems is a fearless account of an inner life of love, frustration, guilt, laughter and the celebration of others. He is best known to the general public as the author of the controversial and bestselling *Hardy* (1994).
1994 • 52 pages • ISBN 1-871551-08-0